# GENERAL KNOWLEDGE QUIZZES for Clever Kids

Written by Joe Fullman
Illustrations and cover
artwork by Chris Dickason

Design and layout by Zoe Bradley and Joe Fullman
Edited by Josephine Southon
Cover Design by Angie Allison
Educational Consultancy by Kirstin Swanson

# GENERAL KNOWLEDGE QUIZZES for Clever Kids

BUSTER BOOKS

First published in Great Britain in 2021 by Buster Books,
an imprint of Michael O'Mara Books Limited,
9 Lion Yard, Tremadoc Road, London SW4 7NQ

W   www.mombooks.com/buster

f   Buster Books

y   @BusterBooks

O   @buster_books

Clever Kids is a trade mark of Michael O'Mara Books Limited.

Illustrations and layouts © Buster Books 2021

A CIP catalogue record for this book is available from the British Library.

ISBN: 978-1-78055-710-6

3 5 7 9 10 8 6 4 2

This product is made of material from well-managed, FSC®-certified
forests and other controlled sources. The manufacturing processes
conform to the environmental regulations of the country of origin.

Printed and bound in June 2023 by
CPI Group (UK) Ltd, Croydon, CR0 4YY.

MIX
Paper | Supporting
responsible forestry
FSC® C171272

# CONTENTS

# HOW THE QUIZZES WORK ⟶

Get ready to go on a fact-packed journey through the world of general knowledge in this fun-filled quizzing adventure!

In this book you will find ten themed chapters, each with 100 quiz questions, giving a grand total of 1,000 challenging, fun and fascinating questions to put your brain to the test.

There are lots of different types of quiz in this book. Some ask you to decide whether a statement is true or false. Others are multiple choice questions with three possible options, so you can have a guess even if you're not quite sure of the answer. There are also visual quizzes where you have to match up pictures, and others where you need to fill in the blanks or spot a deliberate mistake. Some quizzes are designed for two or more players, so that they can be played with friends and family.

Each chapter ends with an Adults vs Kids quiz with two sets of questions, one for adults to be asked by kids, and one for kids to be asked by adults.

The introduction to each quiz will tell you what you need to do. There's also a space at the top of each page for you to write down how many you got right. If you try the quiz again at a later date, you can see if you can get a better score.

Good luck, and happy quizzing!

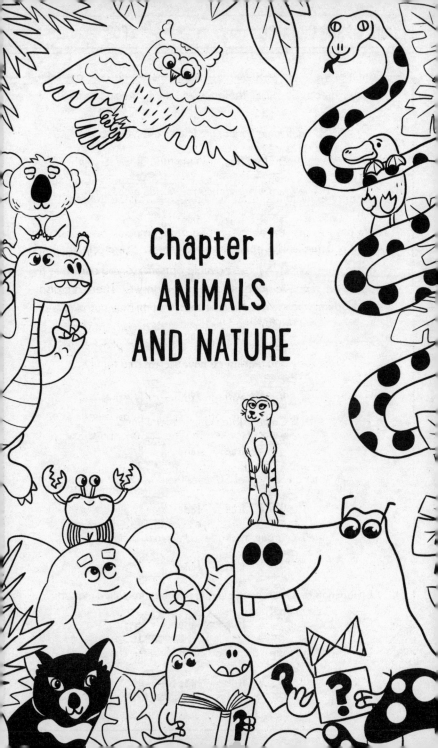

# Chapter 1
# ANIMALS
# AND NATURE

Which of these amazing animal statements are correct, and which are outrageous fibs? Tick the ones you think are true or false.

1. Adult male gorillas are known as silverbacks.

True False

2. The great white shark is the world's biggest fish.

True False

3. In the wild, polar bears live near the South Pole.

True False

4. Sperm whales can hold their breath for an hour and a half.

True False

5. All insects have six legs.

True False

6. Camels store water in their humps.

True False

7. Ants can carry over 50 times their own body weight.

True False

8. A group of giraffes is known as a 'stilt'.

True False

9. Mammals that rear their young in pouches are called marsupials.

True False

10. The fastest animal on Earth is not the cheetah.

True False

For each of these questions, there is just one correct answer.
Circle the correct answer: A, B or C.

1. Growing over 90 m (300 ft) high, the biggest trees on Earth are known
as giant _____?
A) Greenwoods          B) Redwoods          C) Bluewoods

2. What part of their bodies do butterflies use to taste their food?
A) Tongues          B) Feet          C) Wings

3. What is the largest animal that has ever lived?
A) Woolly mammoth     B) *Brachiosaurus*     C) Blue whale

4. What is the world's fastest-running bird?
A) Ostrich          B) Penguin          C) Chicken

5. What do frogs mainly eat?
A) Flowers          B) Insects          C) Jam

6. The world's largest lizard is the Komodo _____?
A) Monster          B) Ogre          C) Dragon

7. What is the name of the fluid that flows through the trunk and branches
of a tree?
A) Nectar          B) Sap          C) Pollen

8. Someone with arachnophobia is afraid of what animals?
A) Spiders          B) Flies          C) Puppies

9. On what continent do wombats live in the wild?
A) Asia          B) Africa          C) Oceania

10. Just 2 cm (0. 8 in) across, what is the world's smallest species of crab?
A) Pea crab          B) Bean crab          C) Corn crab

In each of these nature lists, there's something that doesn't belong. Can you work out what it is? Circle your answers.

**1.** Four of these are fish, but which one is a mammal?

Shark      (Trout)      Tang

Manatee      Salmon

**2.** Which of these animals doesn't live in the wild in Africa?

Hippopotamus      (Meerkat)      Jaguar

Zebra      Giraffe

**3.** Which of these isn't a genuine type of eagle?

Golden eagle      (Hairy eagle)      Bald eagle

Harpy eagle      White-tailed eagle

**4.** Which of these trees is not actually a tree?

Curry tree      Maple tree      Weeping willow tree

Prickly pear tree      (Breadfruit tree)

**5.** Which of these isn't a real type of bear?

Brown bear      Black bear

(Purple bear)      Spectacled bear

Sun bear

**6**. What is the only sea creature you wouldn't see swimming in the waters of Australia's Great Barrier Reef?

Clownfish          Green turtle          Butterflyfish

Angelfish          Walrus

**7**. Which of these animals can't fly?

Barn owl           Vampire bat           Giant centipede

Dragonfly          Bar-headed goose

**8**. Which of these isn't a genuine type of snake?

Anaconda           Boa                   Samba

Asp                Viper

**9**. What is the only country in this list where tigers don't live in the wild?

India              Nepal                 Russia

France             Malaysia

**10**. Which of these animals is not a marsupial?

Kangaroo           Wallaby               Koala

Camel              Tasmanian devil

For each of these questions, there are two correct statements and one incorrect one. Can you work out which is which? Circle the one you think is a mistake.

### 1. SHARK SAVVY
**A)** A great white shark can grow over 6 m (19 ft) long.
**B)** A great white shark has over 300 teeth.
**C)** A great white shark breathes through a hole in the top of its head.

### 2. KOALA KWIZZING
**A)** Koalas feed mainly on leaves.
**B)** Koalas are a type of small bear.
**C)** Koalas can spend up to 22 hours a day asleep.

### 3. LEOPARD LEARNING
**A)** Leopards can change their spots.
**B)** Leopards are found living in the wild in both Africa and Asia.
**C)** Leopards can climb trees.

### 4. GIRAFFE GUESSES
**A)** Giraffes are the tallest land animals.
**B)** Giraffes have purple-coloured tongues.
**C)** Giraffes have four horns on their heads.

### 5. INSECT INFORMATION
**A)** Some species of bee make honey.
**B)** Some species of wasp make mustard.
**C)** Some species of ant farm fungus.

## 6. NAMING NOTIONS
**A)** The horns of a rhinoceros are known as sharpies.
**B)** The long, sharp teeth of a cat are known as fangs.
**C)** The claws of a bird of prey are known as talons.

## 7. MARSUPIAL MYSTERIES
**A)** The largest species of marsupial is the red kangaroo.
**B)** There are just six species of marsupial.
**C)** Some species of marsupial live in North America.

## 8. ANIMAL ANTICS
**A)** The platypus is a mammal that lays eggs.
**B)** Horses can sleep standing up.
**C)** Bulls are angered by the colour red.

## 9. HOME HELP
**A)** A squirrel's home is called a drey.
**B)** A tiger's home is called a snarl.
**C)** An otter's home is called a holt.

## 10. CHAMELEON CONUNDRUMS
**A)** A chameleon's tongue can be twice as long as its body.
**B)** A chameleon's eyes can move independently of one another.
**C)** A chameleon can change colour to match its surroundings.

Each of these ten lists is made up of animals from one of the groups below. Can you work out which is which? Figure out what the animals have in common, then write your answers in the spaces provided.

SHARKS    BIG CATS    SEALS    SEA TURTLES    LIZARDS

SEABIRDS    PENGUINS    BATS    MONKEYS    BIRDS OF PREY

### LIST 1

Lion    Lynx    Jaguar    Puma    Leopard

Group Big cats

### LIST 2

Mandrill    Baboon    Marmoset    Macaque    Tamarin

Group monkeys.

### LIST 3

Tern    Cormorant    Puffin    Pelican    Albatross

Group birds of prey    seabirds

### LIST 4

Gila Monster    Skink    Iguana

Gecko    Slow worm

Group Lizards

### LIST 5

Horseshoe    Fruit    Mouse-eared

Vampire    Whiskered

Group Seals

**LIST 6**   Mako   Blue   Whale   Tiger   Bull

Group *Sharks*

**LIST 7**   Osprey   Golden eagle   Goshawk   Barn owl   Kestrel

Group *Birds osprey*

**LIST 8**   Emperor   Adélie   Chinstrap   Gentoo   Rockhopper

Group *Penguins*

**LIST 9**   Loggerhead   Leatherback   Olive ridley
Green   Hawksbill

Group *Sea turtles*

**LIST 10**   Harp   Elephant   Crabeater   Ringed   Leopard

Group *Seals*

Match each animal to the continent where it lives in the wild. Write your answers in the spaces next to the animals. Each animal lives on no more than one continent.

1. Goliath birdeater spider

REGION ..... *Asapu*

2. Emperor penguin

REGION ..... *A niatic*

3. Orangutan

REGION ..... *Agrica*

4. Black bear

REGION ..... *Asia*

5. Red kangaroo

REGION ..... *Agrica*

6. Panda

REGION ..... *Asia*

NORTH AMERICA

SOUTH AMERICA

7. Bald eagle

REGION Africa

8. Meerkat

REGION Asia

9. Platypus

REGION Asia

EUROPE

ASIA

AFRICA

OCEANIA

10. Green anaconda

REGION Asia

ANTARCTICA

Can you pick out the right answer from the two wrong ones in this multiple choice quiz?

**1.** Living for over 200 years, the world's longest-lived mammal is a type of what?

**A)** Whale　　　　**B)** Monkey　　　　**C)** Dog

**2.** About the size of a dinner plate, the largest eye on Earth belongs to which animal?

**A)** Ostrich　　　　**B)** Walrus　　　　**C)** Giant squid

**3.** From how far away can a howler monkey's howl be heard?

**A)** 2 km (1 mile)　　**B)** 5 km (3 miles)　　**C)** 10 km (6 miles)

**4.** What do pandas mainly eat?

**A)** Bamboo　　　　**B)** Hamburgers　　　　**C)** Insects

**5.** What is a baby horse called?

**A)** Cub　　　　**B)** Foal　　　　**C)** Calf

**6.** What is the world's largest reptile?

**A)** Spitting cobra　　**B)** Green iguana　　**C)** Saltwater crocodile

**7.** What is the world's smallest dog breed?

**A)** Chihuahua　　　**B)** Labrador　　　**C)** Beagle

**8.** What is the only type of bird that can fly backwards?

**A)** Robin　　　　**B)** Hummingbird　　　**C)** Pigeon

**9.** How many eyes does a spider usually have?

**A)** 2　　　　　**B)** 8　　　　　**C)** 16

**10.** Which of these is a genuine tree?

**A)** Jaguar jigsaw tree
**B)** Monkey puzzle tree
**C)** Koala crossword tree

These questions will test your knowledge of cats — big and small.

**1.** What are baby lions called?

A) Cubs          B) Puppies          C) Squabs

**2.** On average, how many whiskers does a cat have on its face?

A) 4          B) 14          C) 24

**3.** Which of these is the real name of a South American jungle cat?

A) Bossalot          B) Ocelot          C) Crossalot

**4.** What is the only species of cat that can't retract (pull in) its claws?

A) Tiger          B) Cheetah          C) Leopard

**5.** What ancient civilization worshipped cats?

A) Egypt          B) Greece          C) China

**6.** In what country did a pet cat called Tomasso inherit millions when its owner died in 2011?

A) USA          B) South Africa          C) Italy

**7.** What fruit do cats not like the smell of?

A) Oranges          B) Apples          C) Bananas

**8.** On average, how long do pet cats sleep per day?

A) 1 hour          B) 5 hours          C) 15 hours

**9.** The only big cats that can roar are the lion, tiger, jaguar and what else?

A) Lynx          B) Leopard          C) Puma

**10.** Creme Puff, the oldest recorded pet cat, lived to be what age?

A) 18          B) 28          C) 38

This is a game for two or more players. One person reads out the clues and the others try to work out what is being talked about. Add up the points at the end – the player with the most is the winner.

### QUESTION 1.
**Clue 1 (4 points):** I'm an insect that lives in a large colony.
**Clue 2 (3 points):** I have wings and my body is yellow and black.
**Clue 3 (2 points):** The place where I live is called a hive.
**Clue 4 (1 point):** I collect nectar and pollen from flowers to make honey.

### QUESTION 2.
**Clue 1 (4 points):** I'm a type of bird that comes out mainly at night.
**Clue 2 (3 points):** I have very large eyes.
**Clue 3 (2 points):** I feed mainly on small rodents such as mice.
**Clue 4 (1 point):** I can turn my head almost all the way round.

### QUESTION 3.
**Clue 1 (4 points):** I'm a mammal from North America, Europe and Asia.
**Clue 2 (3 points):** I live in a small group called a pack.
**Clue 3 (2 points):** I'm the largest member of the dog family.
**Clue 4 (1 point):** I communicate by howling.

### QUESTION 4.
**Clue 1 (4 points):** I live in the sea, but I walk on legs.
**Clue 2 (3 points):** Species of my type include spider, ghost and robber.
**Clue 3 (2 points):** I have ten legs including two large pincers.
**Clue 4 (1 point):** I walk and swim sideways.

### QUESTION 5.
**Clue 1 (4 points):** I'm a giant four-legged mammal from Africa.
**Clue 2 (3 points):** I spend a lot of my time wallowing in water. My name means 'river horse'.
**Clue 3 (2 points):** I have large, long teeth.
**Clue 4 (1 point):** I can open my mouth over 1.2 metres (47 in) wide.

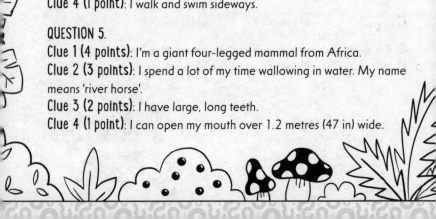

## QUESTION 6.

**Clue 1 (4 points):** I'm a type of bird but I can't fly.

**Clue 2 (3 points):** I mainly eat fish, squid and shellfish.

**Clue 3 (2 points):** I can swim, using my wings like flippers.

**Clue 4 (1 point):** I live near the South Pole where it's very cold.

## QUESTION 7.

**Clue 1 (4 points):** I'm a mammal but I live in the sea.

**Clue 2 (3 points):** I live in a group called a school.

**Clue 3 (2 points):** I communicate using whistles and clicks.

**Clue 4 (1 point):** I often jump out of the sea to perform twists and spins.

## QUESTION 8.

**Clue 1 (4 points):** I'm a type of bird that lives in lakes and lagoons.

**Clue 2 (3 points):** I live in large flocks containing hundreds of birds.

**Clue 3 (2 points):** I have very long legs and a large, curved bill.

**Clue 4 (1 point):** I have bright pink feathers.

## QUESTION 9.

**Clue 1 (4 points):** I'm a hairy animal from the South American jungle.

**Clue 2 (3 points):** I'm as big as a dinner plate.

**Clue 3 (2 points):** I kill prey by injecting it with venom from my fangs.

**Clue 4 (1 point):** I have eight very long legs.

## QUESTION 10.

**Clue 1 (4 points):** I'm a mammal that lives on the African plains.

**Clue 2 (3 points):** I'm a carnivore that both hunts prey and scavenges (eats animals that are already dead).

**Clue 3 (2 points):** I look a bit like a dog.

**Clue 4 (1 point):** I'm famed for my cries which sound a bit like laughter.

Let's see who's smarter, children or adults. The questions at the top are for adults, and should be asked by kids, while the questions down below are for kids, and should be asked by adults. You can ask them all at once or take it in turns.

## QUESTIONS FOR ADULTS

1. What animal has the largest brain of any species?
**A)** African elephant     **B)** Human being     **C)** Sperm whale

2. What is the name for a group of owls?
**A)** Government     **B)** Parliament     **C)** Monarchy

3. What is the world's largest land predator?
**A)** African lion     **B)** Polar bear     **C)** Burmese python

4. Rhinoceros horn is made of bone. True or false?

5. How many eyelids does a dog's eye have?
**A)** One     **B)** Two     **C)** Three

## QUESTIONS FOR KIDS

1. Which bird lays the largest egg?
**A)** Ostrich     **B)** Penguin     **C)** Hummingbird

2. What is the name for a group of lions?
**A)** Courage     **B)** Bravery     **C)** Pride

3. What is the largest land animal?
**A)** Gorilla     **B)** Giraffe     **C)** African elephant

4. All mammals live on land. True or false?

5. How many arms does an octopus have?
**A)** 6     **B)** 8     **C)** 10

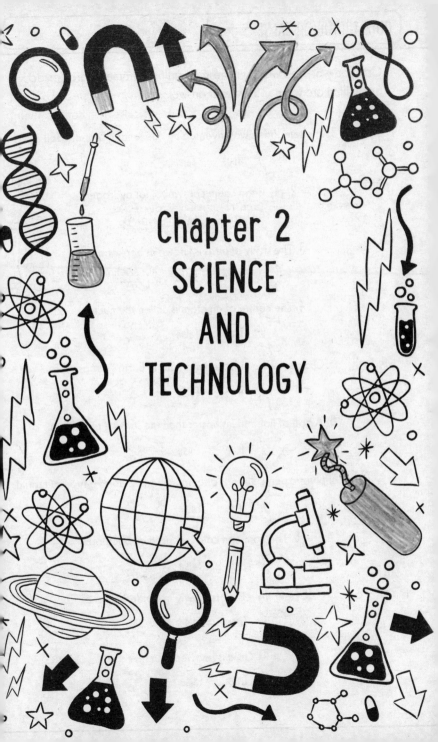

# Chapter 2
# SCIENCE
# AND
# TECHNOLOGY

Can you work out which of these scientific statements are correct, and which are wrong? Tick your answers.

1. The telephone was invented by Alexander Graham Bell.
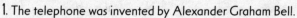 True    False

2. Hy is the chemical symbol for hydrogen.
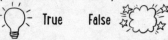 True    False

3. The study of birds is known as beakonology.
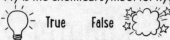 True    False

4. The centre of an atom is called the nucleus.
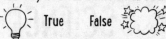 True    False

5. Oxygen is the most common gas in Earth's atmosphere.
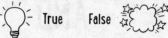 True    False

6. A bolt of lightning is hotter than the surface of the Sun.
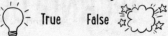 True    False

7. The antibiotic penicillin was originally created using a type of mould.
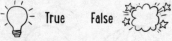 True    False

8. The common cold is caused by bacteria.
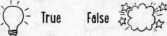 True    False

9. Light travels more slowly in water than in air.
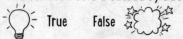 True    False

10. Gold is heavier than silver.
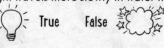 True    False

For each of these questions, there is just one correct answer.
Circle the one you think it is: A, B or C.

1. What is the chemical that gives plants their green colour?
A) Chloroform          B) Chlorophyll          C) Cholesterol

2. In which country was paper invented around 2,000 years ago?
A) USA          B) China          C) India

3. What is the chemical symbol for water?
A) O H          B) $_2$HO          C) $H_2O$

4. In electronics, what does AC stand for?
A) Alternating Current    B) Amplified Current    C) Abra Cadabra

5. A geologist is a scientist who studies what?
A) Trees          B) Rocks          C) Insects

6. In an internet address, what does 'www' stand for?
A) Wi-Fi Wonder Work    B) World Wide Web    C) Wide World Web

7. Solar power generates electricity from what source?
A) Wind          B) Waves          C) The Sun

8. Intense heat and pressure will, over time, turn carbon into what?
A) Diamonds          B) Pearls          C) Emeralds

9. What is a material that carries an electrical charge called?
A) Driver          B) Conductor          C) Ticket collector

10. What is a material that can't carry an electrical charge called?
A) Enveloper          B) Cuddler          C) Insulator

 +  =

In each of these lists, there's something that doesn't belong. Can you work out what it is? Circle your answers.

1. Four of these are metals, but which one is a gas?

Aluminium     Chromium     Helium

Uranium     Platinum

2. Which of these isn't a real science?

Zoology     Farmology     Meteorology

Microbiology     Oceanography

3. Which of these isn't a real type of cloud?

Cumulonimbus     Nimbostratus     Altocumulus

Stratoaltrobus     Cirrostratus

4. Can you spot the rock that's not a rock?

Granite     Pinestone     Basalt

Sandstone     Marble

5. Which of these people isn't a genuine scientist?

Albert Einstein

Marie Curie

Isaac Futon

Galileo Galilei

Nicholaus Copernicus

**6.** Which of these companies doesn't manufacture smartphones?

Apple     Huawei     Chrysler

Samsung     Nokia

**7.** Can you spot the whirlpool among the storms?

Maelstrom     Typhoon     Hurricane

Tornado     Cyclone

**8.** Which of these isn't a genuine type of acid?

Hydrochloric     Sulphuric     Bubonic

Acetic     Nitric

**9.** Which of these is not a layer of the Earth's atmosphere?

Troposphere     Stratosphere     Megasphere

Thermosphere     Exosphere

**10.** Can you spot the unit of length in among the units of electricity?

Watt

Ampere

Nanometre

Volt

Ohm

For each of these questions, there are two correct statements and one incorrect one. Can you work out which is which? Circle the one you think is a mistake.

## 1. KEEP IT LIGHT
**A)** Light is a form of energy.
**B)** The speed of light is very slow – around 3 km (1.8 miles) per hour.
**C)** White light is made up of all the colours of the rainbow.

## 2. STUDYING HARD
**A)** Someone who studies biology is a biologist.
**B)** Someone who studies physics is a physicist.
**C)** Someone who studies chemistry is a zoologist.

## 3. GETTING WARMER
**A)** Seals have warm blood.
**B)** Crocodiles have cold blood.
**C)** Penguins have frozen blood.

## 4. HEARDITALLBIVORE
**A)** An animal that eats meat is a carnivore.
**B)** An animal that eats plants is a verbivore.
**C)** An animal that eats both animals and plants is an omnivore.

## 5. LIGHTNING THE WAY
**A)** Lightning never strikes the same place twice.
**B)** Lightning is a form of electricity.
**C)** Across the world, there are more than three million lightning flashes every day.

## 6. SEE IT THROUGH
**A)** A material that is completely see-through is transparent.
**B)** A material that is partly see-through is translucent.
**C)** A material that cannot be seen through is transpondent.

## 7. WHAT'S IN A NAME?
**A)** The prairie dog is actually a type of cat.
**B)** The flying fox is actually a type of bat.
**C)** The killer whale is actually a type of dolphin.

## 8. DON'T INT-ERUPT
**A)** There are active volcanoes at the bottom of the oceans.
**B)** There are active volcanoes in the sky, floating above the clouds.
**C)** Many islands are the tops of volcanoes that have grown up from the sea floor.

## 9. TRANSPORT TEST
**A)** The plane was invented in Australia.
**B)** The hot-air balloon was invented in France.
**C)** The steam train was invented in Britain.

## 10. GASEOUS GUESSES
**A)** Plants take in carbon dioxide and release oxygen.
**B)** Human beings take in oxygen and release carbon dioxide.
**C)** Cows take in methane and release nitrogen.

Can you write in the word, or words, that are missing from these statements? For each, the correct answer is one of the options in the box to the side.

Soil    Trees

Grass   Flowers

1. Most paper is made from ....................

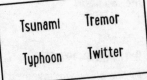

Steam    Commuter

Maglev   Rocket

2. A .................... train uses magnets to hover above the track and travel at super speeds.

Tsunami    Tremor

Typhoon    Twitter

3. A .................... is a giant wave caused by an undersea earthquake.

Core    Centre

Mantle    Crust

4. The .................... is the outermost layer of the Earth.

5. When water is heated it ...................., becoming a gas.

Freezes
Evaporates
Condenses
Transpires

6. The precious stone ..................... is usually coloured green.

Ruby          Sapphire

Diamond       Emerald

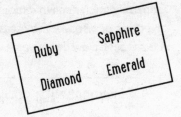

Oxygen    Nitrogen

Hydrogen    Carbon

7. The gas ..................... is the most common substance in the Universe.

1 year        5 years

50 years      1,500 years

8. A plastic bag takes up to ..................... to decompose.

Expand    Contract

Explode    Crumble

9. Metals ..................... when cooled.

Venus fly trap
Saturn bug catcher
Mars minibeast muncher
Jupiter insect gobbler

10. The ..................... is a plant that eats insects.

Can you match each inventor or scientist in the list below to their invention or discovery? Write who you think discovered what in the spaces below the pictures.

### INVENTORS AND SCIENTISTS

| | |
|---|---|
| Karl Benz | Wright Brothers |
| Thomas Edison | Alfred Nobel |
| John Harvey Kellogg | Johannes Gutenberg |
| Marie Curie | Tim Berners-Lee |
| John Logie Baird | Mary Anning |

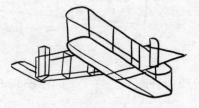

**1. AEROPLANE**

INVENTOR

......................................

**2. TELEVISION**

INVENTOR

......................................

**3. CEREAL FLAKES**

INVENTOR

......................................

**4. MOTOR CAR**

INVENTOR

......................................

**5. LIGHT BULB**

INVENTOR

.................................

**6. *ICHTHYOSAURUS***

DISCOVERER

.................................

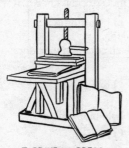

**7. PRINTING PRESS**

INVENTOR

.................................

**8. DYNAMITE**

INVENTOR

.................................

**9. RADIUM AND POLONIUM**

DISCOVERER

.................................

**10. WORLD WIDE WEB**

INVENTOR

.................................

Can you pick out the right answer from the two wrong ones in this multiple choice quiz?

1. What is the name of force that causes things to fall when you drop them?
A) Friction          B) Magnetism          C) Gravity

2. What does a seismologist study?
A) Sizes          B) Earthquakes          C) Dinosaurs

3. What was Albert Einstein's famous equation?
A) $C = E^2M$          B) $MC = E^2$          C) $E = MC^2$

4. The process by which plants use sunlight to make food is known as what?
A) Photosynthesis          B) Parenthesis          C) Hypothesis

5. Sodium chloride is the scientific name for which common substance, which you might put on your food?
A) Ketchup          B) Pepper          C) Salt

6. What is the thin wire inside an incandescent light bulb called?
A) Filbert          B) Filament          C) Filtrum

7. Which of these is a type of rock formed by volcanic eruptions?
A) Sedimentary          B) Igneous          C) Metamorphic

8. A blue whale's heart is about as big as a what?
A) Marble          B) Basketball          C) Motorbike

9. What are the names for the poles on a magnet?
A) Up and Down          B) North and South          C) In and Out

10. What are the thin rocks that rise up from cave floors called?
A) Stalactites          B) Stalagmites          C) Dynamites

Time to get counting. Every answer in this quiz is a number. Pick the one you think is correct.

1. Roughly how long does it take light from the Sun to reach Earth?

A) 8 minutes          B) 8 days          C) 8 weeks

2. In what century was the camera invented?

A) 19th          B) 20th          C) 21st

3. How many megabytes are there in a gigabyte?

A) 10          B) 100          C) 1,000

4. What percentage of a cucumber is water?

A) 5%          B) 50%          C) 95%

5. How many millions of years old are the oldest rocks on Earth?

A) 4.4          B) 440          C) 4,400

6. Today there are over a billion websites. How many were there in 1991?

A) 1          B) 1,000          C) 1 million

7. What number is neutral on the pH scale, so neither acid nor alkaline?

A) 1          B) 7          C) 14

8. Which of these numbers corresponds to the mathematical number pi, used for working out the area and circumference of a circle?

A) 4.13          B) 3.14          C) 1.43

9. In what year was the hand-held mobile (cell) phone invented?

A) 1873          B) 1973          C) 2003

10. Set by the rocket car *ThrustSSC* in 1997, what is the land-speed record?

A) 122.7 kph (76.2 mph)

B) 1,227 kph (762.4 mph)

C) 12,270 kph (7,624.2 mph)

This is a game for two or more players. One person reads out
the clues and the others try to work out what is being talked about.
Add up the points at the end – the player with the most is the winner.

### QUESTION 1.
**Clue 1 (4 points):** I'm a material made from sand, sodium oxide and lime.
**Clue 2 (3 points):** I'm made by being heated and then cooled.
**Clue 3 (2 points):** I can be rolled flat or blown into different shapes.
**Clue 4 (1 point):** I'm used for making window panes, bottles and jars.

### QUESTION 2.
**Clue 1 (4 points):** I'm a device that's found in lots of homes and offices.
**Clue 2 (3 points):** I can be used to store large amounts of information.
**Clue 3 (2 points):** I'm an electronic machine used for solving problems.
**Clue 4 (1 point):** I often come with a screen, keyboard and mouse.

### QUESTION 3.
**Clue 1 (4 points):** I'm a completely see-through substance.
**Clue 2 (3 points):** I'm everywhere you look but you never see me.
**Clue 3 (2 points):** I'm made up of several gases.
**Clue 4 (1 point):** You breathe me in and out all day long.

### QUESTION 4.
**Clue 1 (4 points):** I'm a material that is usually quite hard.
**Clue 2 (3 points):** I can also be very shiny.
**Clue 3 (2 points):** I can be used to make lots of different things, from knives
and forks to cars.
**Clue 4 (1 point):** My types include iron, copper, silver and gold.

### QUESTION 5.
**Clue 1 (4 points):** Born in 1879 in Germany, I grew up to become one of
the most famous scientists in the world.
**Clue 2 (3 points):** I developed the theory of relativity.
**Clue 3 (2 points):** Many people think I was a genius.
**Clue 4 (1 point):** I had long, white hair that stuck out all over the place.

## QUESTION 6.
**Clue 1 (4 points):** I'm everywhere you look, but I'm too small to see.
**Clue 2 (3 points):** There are lots of me in you.
**Clue 3 (2 points):** I'm the smallest part of an element.
**Clue 4 (1 point):** Everything in the Universe is made up
of lots and lots of versions of me.

## QUESTION 7.
**Clue 1 (4 points):** I'm a small, naturally occurring object.
**Clue 2 (3 points):** Trees and plants have lots of me.
**Clue 3 (2 points):** I'm often covered in something that people
and animals find tasty to eat.
**Clue 4 (1 point):** If planted, I'll grow into a new tree or plant.

## QUESTION 8.
**Clue 1 (4 points):** I'm an object that helps other objects work, from cars
to phones.
**Clue 2 (3 points):** I'm usually hidden away, out of sight.
**Clue 3 (2 points):** I can be full or empty.
**Clue 4 (1 point):** When I run out of energy you may have to replace me
or recharge me.

## QUESTION 9.
**Clue 1 (4 points):** There are lots of me in you.
**Clue 2 (3 points):** I can only be seen through a microscope.
**Clue 3 (2 points):** Every living organism is made up of versions of me.
Some have just one, others have billions.
**Clue 4 (1 point):** My types include skin, nerve and red-blood.

## QUESTION 10.
**Clue 1 (4 points):** I'm made up mainly of rock, some of which is very hot.
**Clue 2 (3 points):** I'm a giant sphere orbiting the Sun.
**Clue 3 (2 points):** I'm the only planet that supports life.
**Clue 4 (1 point):** You're standing on me right now.

Let's see who's smarter, children or adults. The questions at the top are for adults, and should be asked by kids, while the questions down below are for kids, and should be asked by adults. You can ask them all at once or take it in turns.

### QUESTIONS FOR ADULTS

1. The Russian aviation pioneer, Igor Sikorsky, invented what type of flying machine in 1939?
A) Aeroplane      B) Helicopter      C) Rocket

2. What is the name for the group of colourless, odourless and largely unreactive gases?
A) Noble gases      B) Royal gases      C) Aristocratic gases

3. Which of these is not a real scientific term for energy?
A) Kinetic      B) Potential      C) Intense

4. The whirlpool bath was invented by Candido Jacuzzi. True or false?

5. What do you call a scientist who studies the weather?
A) Anthropologist      B) Meteorologist      C) Geneticist

### QUESTIONS FOR KIDS

1. The French Montgolfier brothers invented what type of flying machine in 1783?
A) Rocket      B) Hot-air balloon      C) Aeroplane

2. What is the name of the table where all the elements are displayed?
A) Periodic Table      B) Episodic Table      C) Occasional Table

3. The area of San Francisco where there are lots of technology companies is known as _____ Valley?
A) Carbon      B) Lithium      C) Silicon

4. The computer was invented by Charles Cabbage. True or false?

5. What do you call a scientist who studies plants?
A) Plantologist      B) Botanist      C) Paleontologist

# Chapter 3
# SPACE

Tick whether you think these Solar System facts are true or false.

1. There are seven planets in the Solar System.

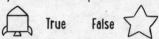 True   False

2. Mercury is the smallest planet in the Solar System.

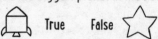 True   False

3. Earth is the biggest planet in the Solar System.

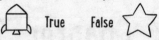 True   False

4. Neptune is the furthest planet from the Sun.

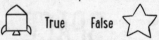 True   False

5. Venus is the coldest planet in the Solar System.

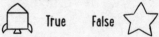 True   False

6. Saturn is the only planet in the Solar System with rings.

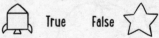 True   False

7. The Great Red Spot on Jupiter is a storm that's bigger than Earth.

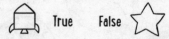 True   False

8. The tallest mountain in the Solar System is on the planet Mars.

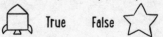 True   False

9. The Sun is made up mainly of lava.

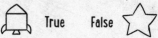 True   False

10. All comets come from the planet Uranus.

True   False

For each of these questions, there is just one correct answer.
Circle the correct answer: A, B or C.

**1.** In what year did people first walk on the Moon?
A) 1869          B) 1969          C) 2009

**2.** The surface of the Moon is covered in what?
A) Craters          B) Trees          C) Rivers

**3.** What is the name of the first person to walk on the Moon?
A) Buzz Aldrin          B) Eugene Cernan          C) Neil Armstrong

**4.** What was the mission that put the first people on the Moon called?
A) Athena          B) Apollo          C) Zeus

**5.** The large flat areas of solid lava on the Moon are known as _____?
A) Forests          B) Seas          C) Deserts

**6.** What sport did the astronaut Alan Shepard play on the Moon?
A) Baseball          B) Basketball          C) Golf

**7.** In total, how many people have walked on the Moon?
A) Two          B) Six          C) Twelve

**8.** The first lunar module on the Moon was named after which bird?
A) Eagle          B) Albatross          C) Sparrow

**9.** The first person on the Moon called it a 'giant leap' for _____?
A) Dogs          B) Mankind          C) Robots

**10.** Roughly, how far is the Moon from Earth?
A) 3,850 km (2,392 miles)
B) 38,500 km (23,923 miles)
C) 385,000 km (239,228 miles)

In each of these lists, there's something that doesn't belong.
Can you work out what it is? Circle your answers.

**1.** Four of the these are planets, but which one is a moon?

Uranus            Neptune            Europa

Saturn            Jupiter

**2.** Which of these isn't a real constellation of the zodiac?

Sagittarius        Aries              Gemini

Tigris            Capricorn

**3.** Which of these isn't a genuine type of star?

Red giant          White dwarf        Blue giant

Yellow dwarf       Green giant

**4.** Which word wouldn't you normally associate with a telescope?

Lens              Keyboard           Focus

Eyepiece          Mirror

**5.** Which of these isn't a
layer of Earth?

Peel              Crust

Mantle            Outer core

Inner core

**6**. Which of these isn't a real astronomical object?

Galaxy            Supernova         Black hole

Death Star        Nebula

**7**. Which of these isn't a genuine spacecraft?

*Sputnik 1*       *Vostok 1*        Space Shuttle *Atlantis*

USS *Enterprise*  *Voyager 1*

**8**. Four of these are rocky planets, but which one is a gas giant?

Mercury           Venus             Earth

Mars              Saturn

**9**. What term would you not normally associate with a spaceflight?

Countdown         Lift-off          U-turn

Orbit             Re-entry

**10**. Can you spot the dwarf planet among the stars?

Sirius            The Sun           Rigel

Pluto             Betelgeuse

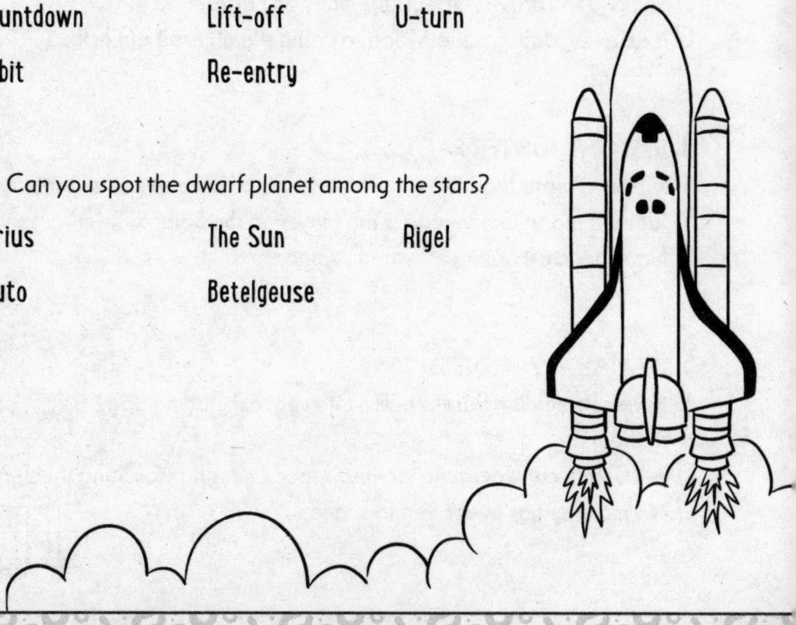

For each of these questions, there are two correct statements and one incorrect one. Can you work out which is which? Circle the one you think is a mistake.

## 1. STAY IN THE SUN
A) Everything in the Solar System orbits the Sun.
B) The Sun contains over 99% of the Solar System's mass.
C) The Sun turns black at night.

## 2. VENUSIAN VITAL STATISTICS
A) Temperatures on Venus can reach over 470°C.
B) Venus has two moons.
C) Venus's clouds are made of sulphuric acid.

## 3. MOON MATTERS
A) The Moon has a thick atmosphere.
B) The Moon's gravity affects the tides on Earth.
C) It takes 27 days for the Moon to complete an orbit of Earth.

## 4. JUST THE JUPITER FACTS
A) Jupiter is more than twice as large as all the other planets combined.
B) Jupiter's moon Ganymede is the largest in the Solar System.
C) No spacecraft have yet visited Jupiter.

## 5. SPATIAL AWARENESS
A) Several animals have travelled into space including dogs, frogs and spiders.
B) In 2018, a car was launched into space and is now orbiting the Sun.
C) No monkey has ever been to space.

## 6. STAR TURN

**A)** There are around 2,000 stars in the Universe.

**B)** All stars eventually run out of fuel and stop burning.

**C)** Very large stars blow up in giant explosions known as supernovas.

## 7. NEPTUNIAN NOTES

**A)** A year on Neptune lasts 165 Earth years.

**B)** The gases in Neptune's atmosphere give it a pinky colour.

**C)** Neptune's winds are the strongest in the Solar System.

## 8. MERCURIOSITY

**A)** You would weigh around a third less on Mercury than you do on Earth.

**B)** It can get very cold on Mercury at night.

**C)** Mercury produces its own light, making it one of the brightest objects in the night sky.

## 9. SENSE TEST

**A)** Sound can travel through empty space.

**B)** Smells can travel through empty space.

**C)** Light can travel through empty space.

## 10. MARTIAN MISSIONS

**A)** There have been more missions to Mars than to any other planet.

**B)** Mars is home to the Solar System's deepest lake.

**C)** Wheeled robots called rovers have explored the Martian surface.

# QUIZ 5: FILL IN THE BLANKS

Can you write in the word, or words, that are missing from these statements? For each statement, the correct answer is one of the options in the box at the side.

1. Mars is known as the .................... planet.

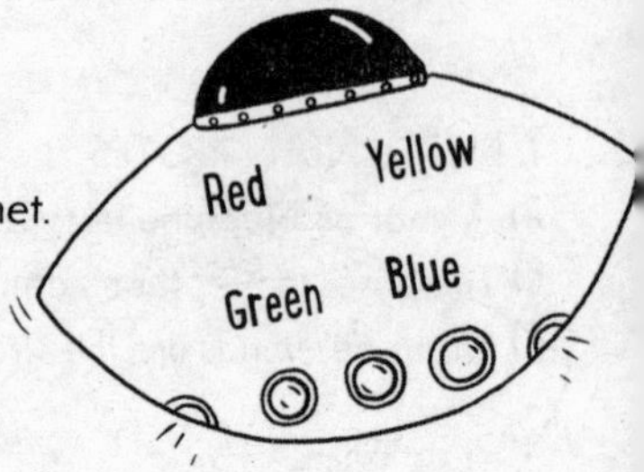

Red
Yellow
Green
Blue

Magnetism    Gravity
Electricity    Muscularity

2. .................... is the force that holds all the planets in orbit round the Sun.

3. .................... was the name of the rocket that launched the first people to the Moon.

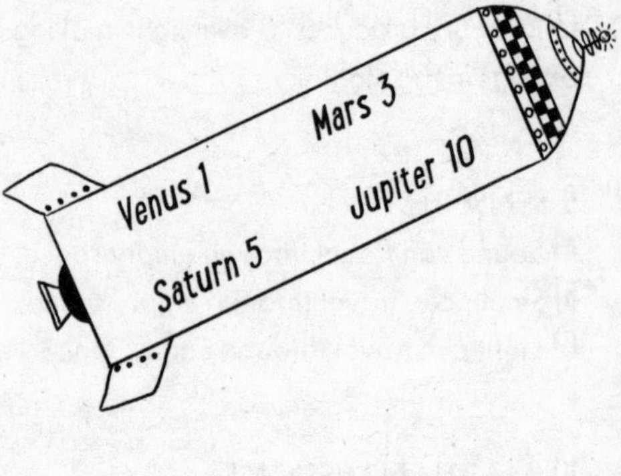

Mars 3
Venus 1
Jupiter 10
Saturn 5

Silk Road    Coffee Path
Tea Street    Milky Way

4. The .................... galaxy contains our solar system.

5. The planet .................... is named after the Roman goddess of love.

Venus    Earth
Mars    Jupiter

**6**. The moment that the Universe began is called the

........................

Colossal Crash

Tremendous Thump

Big Bang

Super Slam

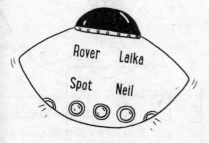

Rover    Laika

Spot    Neil

**7**. ........................ was the name of the first dog to travel into Space.

Mercury    Venus

Earth    Mars

**8**. Over 70% of the planet ........................ is covered in water.

USA    France

Russia    China

**9**. The first person to travel into space was from

........................

**10**. ........................ comet visits Earth every 76 years.

Galileo's    Newton's

Valley's    Halley's

Can you match the names of the Solar System objects to the astronomical bodies in this diagram? Write your answers in the spaces next to the correct picture.

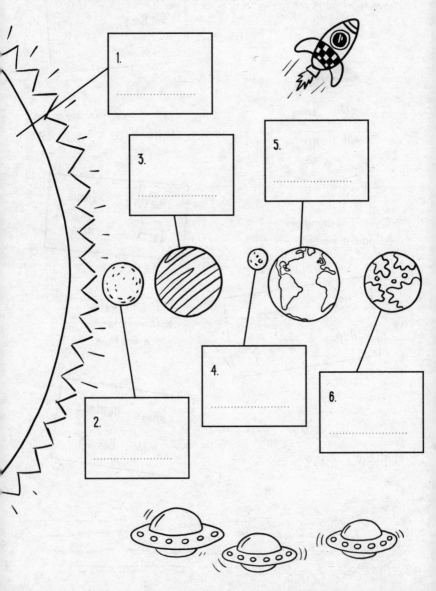

1. .........................

3. .........................

5. .........................

4. .........................

2. .........................

6. .........................

SOLAR SYSTEM OBJECTS

| | |
|---|---|
| The Moon | Mars |
| Neptune | The Sun |
| Mercury | Uranus |
| Saturn | Venus |
| Jupiter | Earth |

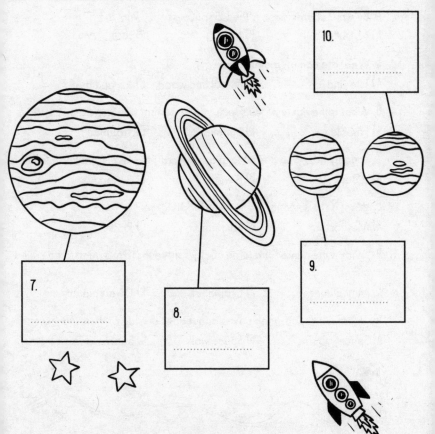

7. ..........................

8. ..........................

9. ..........................

10. ..........................

Can you pick out the right answer from the two wrong ones in this multiple choice quiz?

1. What was the name of the first person to travel into Space?
A) John Glenn        B) Yuri Gagarin        C) H. G. Wells

2. In what year did the first manned spaceflight take place?
A) 1861        B) 1961        C) 2001

3. What is the name of the astronomical object that has such powerful gravity that nothing can escape it, not even light?
A) White dwarf        B) Yellow stone        C) Black hole

4. By what abbreviation is the US space agency known?
A) NASA        B) NATO        C) NODDY

5. What are comets mainly made of?
A) Fire and ice        B) Metal and wood        C) Ice and dust

6. What is the name of the space telescope that was launched in 1990?
A) Hubble        B) Bubble        C) Trouble

7. Roughly how long does it take a spacecraft to travel from Earth to Mars?
A) 8 days        B) 8 weeks        C) 8 months

8. What is the scientific name for a shooting star?
A) Meteor        B) Satellite        C) Rocket

9. What is the name for a large, rocky sphere that's too small to be called a planet?
A) Mini planet        B) Exoplanet        C) Dwarf planet

10. What is it called when an astronaut goes outside of their spacecraft?
A) Space job        B) Space walk        C) Space dance

Are these statements true or false? Tick your answers.

1. The Moon always shows the same side to Earth.

    True    False

2. Uranus is smaller than Earth.

    True    False

3. Earth is the only planet known to support life.

    True    False

4. Mars has three moons.

    True    False

5. In Russia, astronauts are called 'cosmonauts'.

    True    False

6. Valentina Tereshkova was the first woman to travel into space.

    True    False

7. The first manned spaceflight to reach the Moon was Apollo 1.

    True    False

8. Astronauts can grow up to 3% taller in space.

    True    False

9. Mars doesn't have an atmosphere.

    True    False

10. Most comets have two tails.

    True    False

This is a game for two or more players. One reads out the clues, while the others try to work out what is being talked about. Add up the points at the end – the player with the most is the winner.

## QUESTION 1.
**Clue 1 (4 points)**: I'm a big, spinning ball of gas.
**Clue 2 (3 points)**: I'm named after the Roman god of agriculture.
**Clue 3 (2 points)**: I'm the second largest planet in the Solar System.
**Clue 4 (1 point)**: I'm famed for the rings round my middle.

## QUESTION 2.
**Clue 1 (4 points)**: I'm an American who lived from 1930 to 2012.
**Clue 2 (3 points)**: I served in the navy and became a test pilot.
**Clue 3 (2 points)**: In the 1960s, I became an astronaut for NASA's Apollo space programme.
**Clue 4 (1 point)**: I was the first person to set foot on the Moon.

## QUESTION 3.
**Clue 1 (4 points)**: I'm about 1.4 million km (0.9 million miles) across.
**Clue 2 (3 points)**: I sometimes get spots marking cooler areas on my surface.
**Clue 3 (2 points)**: I'm a huge ball of burning gas.
**Clue 4 (1 point)**: You see me every day in the sky.

## QUESTION 4.
**Clue 1 (4 points)**: I'm a large rock a long way from the Sun.
**Clue 2 (3 points)**: I was discovered in 1930.
**Clue 3 (2 points)**: I used to be a planet, but in 2006 I was downgraded to a dwarf planet.
**Clue 4 (1 point)**: I share my name with a cartoon dog.

## QUESTION 5.
**Clue 1 (4 points)**: I'm an item of astronomical equipment.
**Clue 2 (3 points)**: I was invented in the early 17th century and I was used by the Italian scientist Galileo.
**Clue 3 (2 points)**: I'm shaped like a long tube.
**Clue 4 (1 point)**: I make faraway things appear close-up.

## QUESTION 6.

Clue 1 (4 points): I, and other things like me, can be seen in the night sky.

Clue 2 (3 points): I'm made up of several different objects.

Clue 3 (2 points): Throughout history, people have made up stories about me.

Clue 4 (1 point): I'm a group of stars. Examples of my type include Orion, Ursa Major and Capricorn.

## QUESTION 7.

Clue 1 (4 points): I'm a ball of rock somewhere in the Solar System.

Clue 2 (3 points): You can see me in the night sky.

Clue 3 (2 points): People used to wonder if I was made of cheese.

Clue 4 (1 point): People landed on me for the first time in 1969.

## QUESTION 8.

Clue 1 (4 points): I'm a vast region of space.

Clue 2 (3 points): I'm named after a drink.

Clue 3 (2 points): Almost everything you can see in the night sky is contained within me.

Clue 4 (1 point): I'm the galaxy that contains the Solar System.

## QUESTION 9.

Clue 1 (4 points): I'm big and round but I'm not in space.

Clue 2 (3 points): There are lots of me on Earth, and even more on the surface of the Moon.

Clue 3 (2 points): I'm made by rocks from space hitting the surface of an astronomical body.

Clue 4 (1 point): I'm shaped like a bowl.

## QUESTION 10.

Clue 1 (4 points): I'm a large machine with a pointed nose.

Clue 2 (3 points): I can travel at great speeds.

Clue 3 (2 points): I launch straight upwards from the ground.

Clue 4 (1 point): I carry spacecraft up into space.

Let's see who's smarter, children or adults. The questions at the top are for adults, and should be asked by kids, while the questions down below are for kids, and should be asked by adults. You can ask them all at once or take it in turns.

## QUESTIONS FOR ADULTS

**1.** The Asteroid Belt is located between which two planets?
**A)** Mercury and Venus    **B)** Earth and Mars    **C)** Mars and Jupiter

**2.** Which planet has the shortest day, lasting just under 10 hours?
**A)** Mercury    **B)** Jupiter    **C)** Neptune

**3.** In what year did the first Space Shuttle launch?
**A)** 1978    **B)** 1981    **C)** 1988

**4.** The first 'A' in NASA stands for 'Aviation'. True or false?

**5.** What's it called when an astronomical body, such as a planet, passes in front of a larger body, such as the Sun, obscuring a small part of it?
**A)** Transit    **B)** Eclipse    **C)** Sunspot

## QUESTIONS FOR KIDS

**1.** What planet is situated between Mercury and Earth?
**A)** Venus    **B)** Mars    **C)** Uranus

**2.** What is the largest planet in the Solar System?
**A)** Mars    **B)** Jupiter    **C)** Neptune

**3.** In what year was the first artificial satellite, *Sputnik 1*, launched?
**A)** 1927    **B)** 1957    **C)** 1977

**4.** ISS stands for 'International Space Station'. True or false?

**5.** What's it called when an astronomical body, such as the Moon, passes in front of another one, such as the Sun, completely obscuring it?
**A)** Solstice    **B)** Equinox    **C)** Eclipse

# Chapter 4
# HISTORY

Tick whether you think these historical facts are true or false.

1. Henry VIII of England had eight wives.

True    False

2. Jesse Owens won four gold medals at the 1936 Olympics in Berlin.

True    False

3. A samurai was a warrior in medieval China.

True    False

4. The giant ship *Titanic* sank when it hit an iceberg on its first voyage.

True    False

5. A gladiator was a type of cook in ancient Rome.

True    False

6. George Washington was the first president of the USA.

True    False

7. The motor car was invented in the 20th century.

True    False

8. The Pilgrim Fathers' boat was called the *Mayflower*.

True    False

9. World War I began in 1912.

True    False

10. The Vikings came from Scandinavia.

True    False

For each of these questions, there is just one correct answer.
Circle the correct answer: A, B or C.

1. What is the correct name for a pirate flag?
A) Grumpy Sean          B) Jolly Roger          C) Relaxed Katy

2. The ancient general Hannibal marched which animals across the Alps?
A) Tigers               B) Kangaroos            C) Elephants

3. Who was the thunderbolt-throwing king of the Greek gods?
A) Zeus                 B) Apollo               C) Poseidon

4. What is the aeroplane used by the President of the USA called?
A) White House One      B) Air Force One        C) President One

5. The 5th-century warrior who battled the Romans was Attila the _____?
A) Fun                  B) Bun                  C) Hun

6. Issued in 1840, the world's first postage stamp was the _____?
A) Penny Black          B) Twopence Blue        C) Dollar Red

7. According to the legends, what shape was King Arthur's table?
A) Round                B) Square               C) Triangular

8. What do Aboriginal Australians call the time of the Earth's creation?
A) The Sleeptime        B) The Dreamtime        C) The Night-time

9. What age came between the Stone Age and the Iron Age?
A) The Gold Age         B) The Silver Age       C) The Bronze Age

10. What was the name of the last pharaoh of ancient Egypt?
A) Nefertiti            B) Cleopatra            C) Cominatya

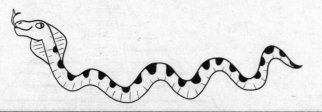

In each of these lists, there's something that doesn't belong.
Can you spot what it is? Circle your answers.

1. Four of these are Roman gods and goddesses, but which one is a
Norse god?

Jupiter          Venus          Odin

Neptune          Apollo

2. Which of these is a British prime minister and not a US president?

Thomas Jefferson     Abraham Lincoln     Theodore Roosevelt

Winston Churchill    John F. Kennedy

3. Which of these is not a commonly used term for a historical period?

Outer Ages       Middle Ages    Renaissance

Great Depression  Space Age

4. Which of these wasn't an Egyptian pharaoh?

Ramses           Julius Caesar   Thutmose

Amenhotep        Tutankhamun

5. Which of these were not one of the
ancient peoples of Mexico?

Olmecs           Maya

Toltecs          Aztecs

Saxons

**6**. Which of these isn't an ancient Greek philosopher?

Plato                Socrates                Aristotle

Newton               Archimedes


**7**. Which of these wasn't crowned a king of England?

Richard III          George VI               Edward VIII

James III            Stephen


**8**. Can you identify the fake prehistoric mammal?

Cave bear            Horned beaver           Sabre-toothed cat

Mammoth              Woolly rhino


**9**. Which of these wasn't a genuine Chinese dynasty?

Song                 Tang                    King

Ming                 Qing


**10**. Four of these are Roman emperors, but one is an imposter. Do you know which one?

Augustus             Caligula

Zero                 Hadrian

Constantine

For each of these questions, there are two correct statements and one incorrect one. Can you work out which is which? Circle the one you think is a mistake.

## 1. WALL SCHOOL
**A)** The Great Wall of China stretches for over 8,850 km (5,500 miles).
**B)** The wall is so large it's visible from space with the naked eye.
**C)** The earliest sections were built with packed earth rather than stone.

## 2. FIRING QUESTIONS
**A)** The Great Fire of London took place in 1666.
**B)** It started in a bakery on Pudding Lane.
**C)** It ended in a cake shop on Dessert Street.

## 3. RECALLING REVOLUTIONS
**A)** The American Revolution took place in the 18th century.
**B)** The French Revolution took place in the 19th century.
**C)** The Russian Revolution took place in the 20th century.

## 4. CASTLE CONFUSION
**A)** Most medieval castles were built at the bottom of a hill.
**B)** Many medieval castles had thin windows called arrow slits.
**C)** Some castles were surrounded with a water-filled ditch called a moat.

## 5. LEGENDARY LEARNING
**A)** According to legend, King Arthur lived in Camelot castle.
**B)** King Arthur was helped by a wizard called Lancelot.
**C)** King Arthur's magical sword was called Excalibur.

### 6. EXTRAORDINARY EXPLORERS
**A)** The Portuguese sailor Ferdinand Magellan was captain of the first ship to sail all the way around the world.
**B)** The Italian sailor Christopher Columbus was not the first European to reach the Americas.
**C)** The British sailor Captain James Cook was the first person to set foot on Australian soil.

### 7. FIRST CHOICE
**A)** World War I lasted for four years.
**B)** World War I started in Africa.
**C)** The USA entered World War I in 1917.

### 8. IMPERIAL MEASUREMENTS
**A)** Genghis Khan was an emperor of the Mongol Empire.
**B)** Mahatma Gandhi was an emperor of India.
**C)** Napoleon Bonaparte was an emperor of France.

### 9. WAR SCORE
**A)** The Thirty Years War of the 17th century lasted less than 30 years.
**B)** The Seven Years War of the 18th century lasted exactly seven years.
**C)** The Hundred Years War of the 14th and 15th centuries lasted more than 100 years.

### 10. WRITING THE WRONGS
**A)** The writing system of the ancient Greeks is called Corinthian.
**B)** The writing system of the ancient Sumerians is called Cuneiform.
**C)** The writing system of the ancient Egyptians is called Hieroglyphics.

Can you write in the word, or words, that are missing from these statements? For each statement, the correct answer is one of the options written on the scroll.

1. The first tsar of Russia was known as Ivan the ...................

Miserable   Smelly

Terrible   Cruel

Green   Fertile

Sandy   Pleasant

2. The ................... Crescent is where the first civilization emerged in the Middle East.

3. According to legend, the founders of Rome, Romulus and Remus, were raised by a

...................

Lion   Owl

Parrot   Wolf

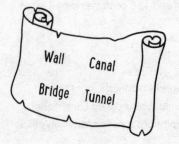

Wall   Canal

Bridge   Tunnel

4. The Berlin ................... divided the German city in two between 1961 and 1989.

5. The British monument Stonehenge is around ................... years old.

50   500

5,000   50,000

**6.** The ..................... War was a political stand-off between the USA and the Soviet Union that lasted from 1945 to 1991.

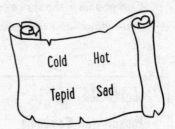

Cold    Hot

Tepid    Sad

Milk    Silk

Wheat    Gold

**7.** The .............. Road was an overland trading route that operated between China and Europe in ancient times.

**8.** In 2009, ................. .................. became president of the United States.

Ronald Reagan

George Bush

Barack Obama

Donald Trump

Turret    Battlement

Keep    Portcullis

**9.** A ..................... was a sliding metal gate at the entrance to a medieval castle.

**10.** The Roman city of ...................... was buried by ash in 79 CE when the volcano Vesuvius erupted.

Pompeii    Milan

Venice    Rome

Can you fill in the spaces on this timeline to show when each of these major landmarks was completed? The pictures are clues.

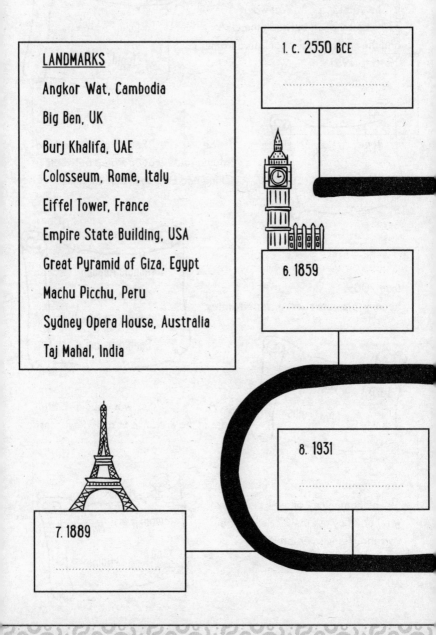

### LANDMARKS

Angkor Wat, Cambodia

Big Ben, UK

Burj Khalifa, UAE

Colosseum, Rome, Italy

Eiffel Tower, France

Empire State Building, USA

Great Pyramid of Giza, Egypt

Machu Picchu, Peru

Sydney Opera House, Australia

Taj Mahal, India

1. c. 2550 BCE

......................

6. 1859

......................

8. 1931

......................

7. 1889

......................

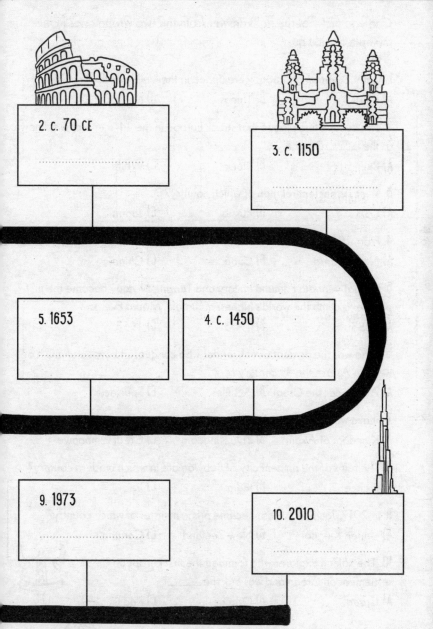

2. c. 70 CE

...........................................

3. c. 1150

...........................................

5. 1653

...........................................

4. c. 1450

...........................................

9. 1973

...........................................

10. 2010

...........................................

Can you pick out the right answer from the two wrong ones in this multiple choice quiz?

1. Many Egyptian pharaohs were buried in the Valley of the _____?
A) Kings          B) Things          C) Mummies

2. The devastating plague that struck Europe in the 14th century was known as the _____ Death?
A) Red          B) Black          C) White

3. Shinto is ancient religion of which country?
A) USA          B) Russia          C) Japan

4. From 1959 to 2008, Fidel Castro was ruler of which communist country?
A) North Korea          B) Cuba          C) China

5. In what year did Edmund Hillary and Tenzing Norgay become the first people to climb the world's highest mountain, Mount Everest?
A) 1853          B) 1903          C) 1953

6. Who was the ancient Greek leader who conquered Egypt and much of western Asia in the 4th century BCE?
A) Alexander the Great   B) Achilles          C) Spartacus

7. Shaka was king of which African kingdom in the 19th century?
A) Kingdom of Axum     B) Zulu Kingdom     C) Great Zimbabwe

8. The ruins of the ancient city of Babylon are in which modern country?
A) France          B) India          C) Iraq

9. In 2017, Jacinda Ardern became prime minister of which country?
A) United Kingdom     B) New Zealand     C) Canada

10. The Viking explorer who founded the first European settlement on Greenland was Erik the _____?
A) Green          B) Orange          C) Red

Are these statements true or false? Tick your answers.

1. The Battle of Hastings took place in 1066.
   True    False

2. Christmas Island is known for its giant stone statues of heads.
   True    False

3. The religion of Islam was founded by the prophet Muhammad.
   True    False

4. England's Great Plague of 1655 was caused by infectious dog bites.
   True    False

5. The Inca Empire was based in South America.
   True    False

6. Sri Lanka used to be known as Ceylon.
   True    False

7. The Italian explorer Marco Polo went to Australia in the Middle Ages.
   True    False

8. The Suez Canal was opened before the Panama Canal.
   True    False

9. World War II ended in 1955.
   True    False

10. Democracy was invented in ancient Greece.
   True    False

This is a game for two or more players. One reads out the clues, while the others try to work out what is being talked about. Add up the points at the end – the player with the most is the winner.

QUESTION 1.
Clue 1 (4 points): I'm a major US politician of the 19th century.
Clue 2 (3 points): I led the North in the American Civil War.
Clue 3 (2 points): I wore a tall hat and had a beard (but no moustache).
Clue 4 (1 point): I signed the declaration that freed enslaved people in my country.

QUESTION 2.
Clue 1 (4 points): I'm a medieval landmark in Italy.
Clue 2 (3 points): I was started in 1173 but not finished till 1372.
Clue 3 (2 points): It looked like I might fall over before I was completed.
Clue 4 (1 point): I'm still standing today, but I lean over severely to one side.

QUESTION 3.
Clue 1 (4 points): I'm a British scientist from the 19th century.
Clue 2 (3 points): I travelled round the world on a ship called HMS *Beagle*.
Clue 3 (2 points): I studied the animals of the Galápagos Islands.
Clue 4 (1 point): I came up with the theory of the evolution of species through natural selection.

QUESTION 4.
Clue 1 (4 points): I'm a major 19th-century landmark in the United States.
Clue 2 (3 points): I was built in France and then shipped to the US.
Clue 3 (2 points): I'm 93 m (305 ft) tall and carry a torch in my right hand.
Clue 4 (1 point): I was erected in New York Harbor.

QUESTION 5.
Clue 1 (4 points): I was an African queen in the 1st century BCE.
Clue 2 (3 points): I formed close relationships with the Roman leaders, Julius Caesar and Marc Anthony.
Clue 3 (2 points): I was one of the few female rulers of Egypt.
Clue 4 (1 point): I was killed by a bite from an asp (a snake).

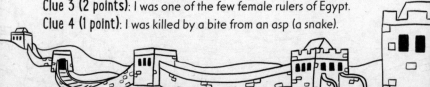

## QUESTION 6.

Clue 1 (4 points): I'm a 20th-century African politician.

Clue 2 (3 points): I campaigned against my country's racist laws.

Clue 3 (2 points): The government put me in prison for 27 years.

Clue 4 (1 point): After my release, I went on to become the first black president of South Africa.

## QUESTION 7.

Clue 1 (4 points): I'm a giant defensive barrier in Asia.

Clue 2 (3 points): I have thousands of watchtowers along my length.

Clue 3 (2 points): I was started over two thousand years ago by my country's first emperor.

Clue 4 (1 point): I was completed during the Ming Dynasty (1368–1644).

## QUESTION 8.

Clue 1 (4 points): I'm a British queen from the 16th century.

Clue 2 (3 points): I succeeded my sister Mary to the throne.

Clue 3 (2 points): I was the daughter of Henry VIII, but I didn't have any children of my own.

Clue 4 (1 point): My navy defeated the Spanish Armada in 1588.

## QUESTION 9.

Clue 1 (4 points): I'm a statue in North Africa made in around 2500 BCE.

Clue 2 (3 points): I stand next to the great pyramids in Egypt.

Clue 3 (2 points): I'm famed for my riddle.

Clue 4 (1 point): I have a human head and the body of a lion.

## QUESTION 10.

Clue 1 (4 points): I'm a 20th-century US civil rights leader.

Clue 2 (3 points): I was named after a 16th-century religious reformer.

Clue 3 (2 points): I won the Nobel Peace Prize in 1964 for my campaign against racial inequality.

Clue 4 (1 point): I delivered a famous speech called 'I have a dream'.

Let's see who's smarter, children or adults. The questions at the top are for adults, and should be asked by kids, while the questions down below are for kids, and should be asked by adults. You can ask them all at once or take it in turns.

## QUESTIONS FOR ADULTS

1. What sort of ships did Vikings travel in?
A) Shortships        B) Midships        C) Longships

2. The Orange Revolution of 2004–05 took place in which country?
A) France        B) Ukraine        C) Russia

3. The uprisings in North Africa and the Middle East in the early 2010s were known as the Arab _____?
A) Spring        B) Summer        C) Winter

4. Bolivia is named after the South American revolutionary Simón Bolívar. True or false?

5. When Columbus arrived in the Americas, where did he think he was?
A) The Americas        B) Asia        C) The North Pole

## QUESTIONS FOR KIDS

1. The traditional rowboats of Venice are known as _____?
A) Vaporetti        B) Coracles        C) Gondolas

2. The Industrial Revolution started in which country?
A) USA        B) UK        C) China

3. The plan to blow up England's parliament in 1605 was the ___ plot?
A) Gunpowder        B) Dynamite        C) TNT

4. America was named after the Italian explorer, Amerigo Vespucci. True or false?

5. What year did Columbus arrive in the Americas for the first time?
A) 492        B) 1492        C) 1942

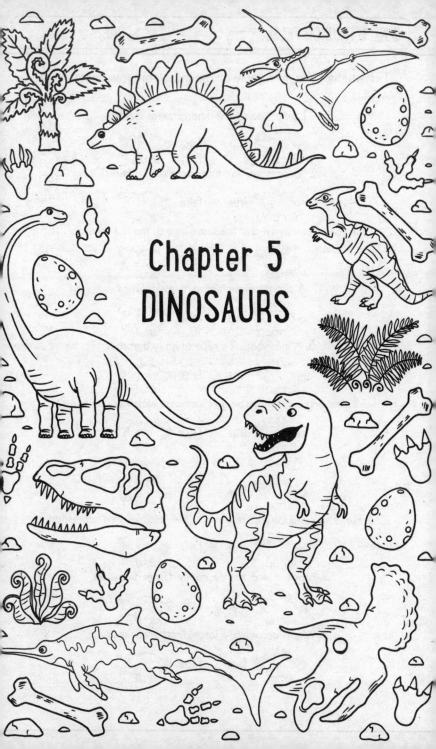

# Chapter 5
# DINOSAURS

Tick whether you think these dinosaur facts are true or false.

1. *Stegosaurus* was a fierce meat-eater.

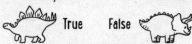 True    False

2. *Triceratops* had three horns on its head.

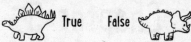 True    False

3. Early humans lived at the same time as the last dinosaurs.

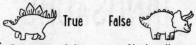 True    False

4. *Brontosaurus* means 'thunder lizard'.

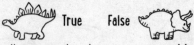 True    False

5. A mammoth is a type of hairy dinosaur.

 True    False

6. The first dinosaur to be given a name was *Megalosaurus*.

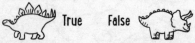 True    False

7. *Ankylosaurus* was the longest dinosaur.

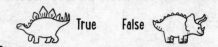 True    False

8. Prehistoric marine reptiles such as *Plesiosaurus* aren't dinosaurs.

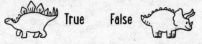 True    False

9. Modern birds are descended from dinosaurs.

True    False

10. *Microraptor* was a large, feathered dinosaur.

True    False

For each of these questions, there is just one correct answer.
Circle the correct answer: A, B or C.

**1.** What sort of creatures were dinosaurs?

**A)** Reptiles        **B)** Mammals        **C)** Amphibians

**2.** *Iguanodon* had a spike on which part of its body?

**A)** Nose        **B)** Thumb        **C)** Tail

**3.** What was the name of the first film about a dinosaur theme park, released in 1993?

**A)** *Jurassic Park*        **B)** *Jurassic World*        **C)** *Jurassic Land*

**4.** Which dinosaur era came first?

**A)** Triassic        **B)** Jurassic        **C)** Cretaceous

**5.** What does the 'rex' in *Tyrannosaurus rex* mean?

**A)** Prince        **B)** Queen        **C)** King

**6.** Dinosaurs with very long necks and tails are known as _____?

**A)** Gastropods        **B)** Sauropods        **C)** Theropods

**7.** A *Diplodocus*'s teeth were shaped like _____?

**A)** Pegs        **B)** Cubes        **C)** Balls

**8.** Which of these three dinosaurs existed first?

**A)** *Stegosaurus*        **B)** *Iguanodon*        **C)** *Tyrannosaurus*

**9.** On what continent did *Allosaurus* live?

**A)** Asia        **B)** Africa        **C)** North America

**10.** Pterosaurs were prehistoric reptiles that could do what?

**A)** Swim        **B)** Fly        **C)** Live underground

In each of these dino lists, there's something that doesn't belong. Can you spot what it is? Circle your answers.

1. Which one is the vegetarian among the meat-eaters?

Tyrannosaurus        Allosaurus        Spinosaurus

Parasaurolophus      Velociraptor

2. Which one is the meat-eater among the herbivores?

Brachiosaurus        Iguanodon         Pachycephalosaurus

Protoceratops        Troodon

3. All of these dinosaurs walked on four legs, except one which walked on two legs. Do you know which one it is?

Ankylosaurus         Giganotosaurus    Stegosaurus

Brontosaurus         Argentinosaurus

4. Can you find the dino that walked on four legs rather than two?

Deinonychus          Baryonyx          Megalosaurus

Microraptor          Diplodocus

5. Which is the only short-necked dinosaur among all of these long-necked giants?

Giraffatitan         Apatosaurus       Triceratops

Camarasaurus         Nigersaurus

**6.** Can you spot the only land-living dinosaur among these prehistoric flying reptiles?

Pterodactyl      Dimorphodon      Pteranodon

Quetzalcoatlus      Tarbosaurus

**7.** Can you identify one giant dinosaur among the small ones?

Compsognathus      Spinosaurus      Microraptor

Archaeopteryx      Coelophysis

**8.** Which one of these films doesn't feature dinosaurs?

Jurassic Park      King Kong      Frozen

Jurassic World      The Land Before Time

**9.** Which is the only genuine dinosaur in among these creatures?

Albertosaurus      Frankosaurus      Isabellasaurus

Bobosaurus      Annasaurus

**10.** Can you spot the only land-living dinosaur among these prehistoric marine reptiles?

Mosasaurus      Ichthyosaurus      Tylosaurus

Hadrosaurus      Pliosaurus

For each of these questions, there are two correct statements and one incorrect one. Can you work out which is which? Circle the one you think is a mistake.

## 1. FASCINATING FOSSILS
**A)** Fossils of dinosaur footprints are known as trace fossils.
**B)** Fossils of dinosaur poos are known as coprolites.
**C)** Fossils of food inside a dinosaur are known as mealalites.

## 2. TIME TEST
**A)** Turtles were around at the same time as the dinosaurs.
**B)** Kangaroos were around at the same time as the dinosaurs.
**C)** Crocodiles were around at the same time as the dinosaurs.

## 3. STEGOSAURUS STUDIES
**A)** *Stegosaurus* had a large brain about the size of a basketball.
**B)** Large, flat plates called 'scutes' ran all the way along its back.
**C)** For defence, it had sharp spikes at the end of its tail.

## 4. ALL ABOUT ANKYLOSAURUS
**A)** *Ankylosaurus* lived in the Jurassic era around 120 million years ago.
**B)** Its body was covered in an armour of hard, bony plates.
**C)** At the end of its tail was a bony club, which it could swing at attackers.

## 5. SUPER SCIENCE
**A)** Dinosaur fossils weren't identified and named until the early 19th century. Before that, no one knew what they were.
**B)** Early dinosaur reconstructions were often inaccurate, with parts put in the wrong place by accident.
**C)** In the early 2000s, scientists managed to bring a dinosaur back to life using DNA recovered from fossils.

## 6. BRACHIOSAURUS BRAINTEASERS

**A)** *Brachiosaurus* could grow as tall as a four-storey building.

**B)** Its name means 'lizard that's as tall as a house'.

**C)** Its nostrils were located on the top of its head.

## 7. ICHTHYOSAURUS INTELLIGENCE

**A)** The name *Icthyosaurus* means 'fish lizard'.

**B)** Although it lived in the sea, it had to come onto land to hunt.

**C)** *Ichthyosaurus* breathed air just like modern whales and dolphins do.

## 8. QUESTIONING QUETZALCOATLUS

**A)** *Quetzalcoatlus* had a wingspan as big as a small plane.

**B)** It was named after the feathered serpent god of the Aztecs.

**C)** It was too big to actually fly and used its wings for swimming instead.

## 9. SIZING THINGS UP

**A)** Giant long-necked dinosaurs called titanosaurs were the largest land animals of all time.

**B)** Giant marine reptiles called mosasaurs were the largest sea creatures of all time.

**C)** Giant two-legged dinosaurs belonging to the theropod group were the largest land predators of all time.

## 10. TERRIBLE TYRANNOSAURUS

**A)** *Tyrannosaurus* lived around 66 million years ago.

**B)** A fully grown adult could be up to 12 m (39 ft) long.

**C)** Baby *Tyrannosaurus* had wings.

Can you write in the word, words or numbers that are missing from these statements? For each statement, the correct answer is one of the options in the box at the side.

1. Dinosaurs died out around ............. million years ago.

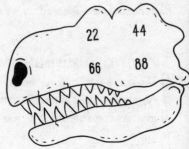

22    44
66    88

Chemistry    Physics

Genetics    Palaeontology

2. ................. is the science of studying fossils and dinosaurs.

3. The word dinosaur means

.................................. .

Giant lizard    Terrible lizard

Long lizard    Friendly lizard

Godzilla    Frankenstein

Dracula    Jabba the Hut

4. ......................... is a Japanese dinosaur-like monster which has appeared in several films.

5. It was around ................... million years ago that the first dinosaurs appeared.

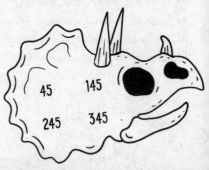

45    145
245    345

**6.** In ancient China, people thought dinosaur fossils were

...............................

| Alien bones | Tiger bones |
| Dragon bones | Tree trunks |

| Australia | Antarctica |
| Europe | North America |

**7.** ........................... is the continent where the largest number of dinosaurs have been discovered.

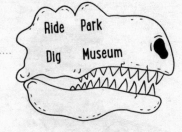

Ride  Park

Dig  Museum

**8.** The first ever dinosaur ........................... was opened to the public in 1854 in the grounds of the Crystal Palace in London.

| Hawaiiraptor | Floridasaurus |
| Utahraptor | Californiasaurus |

**9.** ........................... is a dinosaur named after the US state where it was discovered.

**10.** The first dinosaurs to emerge were

...............................

| Small | Large |
| Winged | Furry |

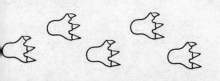

Can you identify these dinosaurs and prehistoric reptiles just from their silhouettes? Write your answers in the spaces.

### DINOSAURS AND REPTILES

Ankylosaurus      Brachiosaurus

Iguanodon         Mosasaurus

Parasaurolophus   Pteranodon

Spinosaurus       Stegosaurus

Tyrannosaurus     Velociraptor

1. .................................

2. .................................

3. .................................

4. .................................

5. .............................

6. .............................

7. .............................

8. .............................

9. .............................

10. .............................

Can you pick out the right answer from the two wrong ones in this multiple choice quiz?

**1.** In what geological period did *Tyrannosaurus* roam the Earth?

**A)** Triassic          **B)** Jurassic          **C)** Cretaceous

**2.** On what continent did *Tyrannosaurus* live?

**A)** North America    **B)** Europe          **C)** Africa

**3.** What does the word '*Tyrannosaurus*' mean?

**A)** Tall lizard       **B)** Tyrant lizard    **C)** Terrific lizard

**4.** How much did a fully grown *Tyrannosaurus* weigh?

**A)** 2,000 kg (4,400 lbs)

**B)** 7,000 kg (15,400 lbs)

**C)** 20,000 kg (44,000 lbs)

**5.** How fast could *Tyrannosaurus* run?

**A)** 20 kph (12 mph)   **B)** 50 kph (31 mph)   **C)** 100 kph (62 mph)

**6.** How long could the teeth of a *Tyrannosaurus* grow?

**A)** 2 cm (0.8 in)     **B)** 20 cm (8 in)     **C)** 200 cm (80 in)

**7.** Which of these meat-eating dinosaurs was even bigger than the fearsome *Tyrannosaurus*?

**A)** *Velociraptor*     **B)** *Deinonychus*    **C)** *Spinosaurus*

**8.** When was the first *Tyrannosaurus* discovered?

**A)** 1852              **B)** 1902            **C)** 1952

**9.** One of the most complete *Tyrannosaurus* fossils is on display in the Field Museum of Natural History in Chicago, USA. What is its name?

**A)** Sarah             **B)** Sue             **C)** Sophia

**10.** Another *Tyrannosaurus* called Stan became the most expensive fossil ever in 2020. How much was it sold for?

**A)** $3.2 million      **B)** $320 million     **C)** $32 million

Are these statements true or false? Tick your answers.

1. Flying insects were around before the dinosaurs.

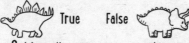 True    False

2. Most dinosaurs were carnivores.

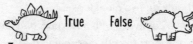 True    False

3. Dinosaurs gave birth to live young.

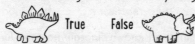 True    False

4. We don't know what colour any dinosaurs were.

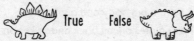 True    False

5. *Diplodocus* lived in the Jurassic Period.

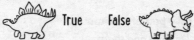 True    False

6. Small mammals were around at the same time as the dinosaurs.

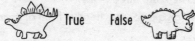 True    False

7. The smallest dinosaur was smaller than a chicken.

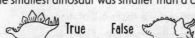 True    False

8. Hadrosaurs were dinosaurs with duck-like bills.

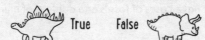 True    False

9. Sauropods had the largest skulls of any dinosaur.

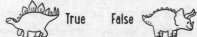 True    False

10. The term 'dinosaur' was invented by the scientist Charles Darwin.

 True    False

This is a game for two or more players. One reads out the clues, while the others try to work out what is being talked about. Add up the points at the end – the player with the most is the winner.

### QUESTION 1.
**Clue 1 (4 points):** I'm a dinosaur from the Cretaceous Period.
**Clue 2 (3 points):** I walk on two giant legs.
**Clue 3 (2 points):** I'm a carnivore with huge jaws and teeth.
**Clue 4 (1 point):** I'm the most famous dinosaur in the world.

### QUESTION 2.
**Clue 1 (4 points):** I'm a well-known dinosaur from the Jurassic Period.
**Clue 2 (3 points):** I live in North America and Western Europe.
**Clue 3 (2 points):** I have a big body and a small head.
**Clue 4 (1 point):** I have plates on my back and spikes on my tail.

### QUESTION 3.
**Clue 1 (4 points):** I'm a part of a dinosaur.
**Clue 2 (3 points):** I'm long and sharp.
**Clue 3 (2 points):** There are three of me.
**Clue 4 (1 point):** I sit on a dinosaur's head in front of its crest.

### QUESTION 4.
**Clue 1 (4 points):** I'm a place that's full of dinosaurs.
**Clue 2 (3 points):** I'm also often full of people.
**Clue 3 (2 points):** The first of my kind opened in the 19th century.
**Clue 4 (1 point):** I have cases of fossils and displays of animatronic models.

### QUESTION 5.
**Clue 1 (4 points):** I'm a period of time from long ago.
**Clue 2 (3 points):** I began around 252 million years ago.
**Clue 3 (2 points):** Dinosaurs first appeared when I was around.
**Clue 4 (1 point):** After around 50 million years, I gave way to the Jurassic Period.

## QUESTION 6.

**Clue 1 (4 points):** I'm a type of herbivorous dinosaur.

**Clue 2 (3 points):** I was one of the earliest dinosaurs to be given a name.

**Clue 3 (2 points):** Sometimes I walk on four legs, sometimes I walk on two.

**Clue 4 (1 point):** I have large spikes on my thumbs.

## QUESTION 7.

**Clue 1 (4 points):** I'm a giant dinosaur from the Cretaceous Period.

**Clue 2 (3 points):** I'm one of the largest dinosaurs to ever have lived.

**Clue 3 (2 points):** I have a long neck and huge, tree-trunk-like legs.

**Clue 4 (1 point):** I'm named after the South American country where I was discovered.

## QUESTION 8.

**Clue 1 (4 points):** I spend a lot of time with dinosaurs.

**Clue 2 (3 points):** I'm a type of scientist.

**Clue 3 (2 points):** I study things that are no longer alive.

**Clue 4 (1 point):** I dig up fossil dinosaurs and help to reconstruct them.

## QUESTION 9.

**Clue 1 (4 points):** I'm a small dinosaur from around 150 million years ago.

**Clue 2 (3 points):** I was discovered in Germany in the mid-19th century.

**Clue 3 (2 points):** I have feathers like a bird and can fly.

**Clue 4 (1 point):** I'm seen as a link between dinosaurs and modern birds.

## QUESTION 10.

**Clue 1 (4 points):** I've spent a long time under the ground.

**Clue 2 (3 points):** I was formed over millions of years.

**Clue 3 (2 points):** I was once a living organism but I was gradually transformed into rock.

**Clue 4 (1 point):** I was recently dug up and put on display in a museum.

Let's see who's smarter, children or adults. The questions at the top are for adults, and should be asked by kids, while the questions at the bottom are for kids, and should be asked by adults. You can ask them all at once or take it in turns.

### QUESTIONS FOR ADULTS

**1.** Which of these is a genuine dinosaur?

**A)** *Annoyor*          **B)** *Irritator*          **C)** *Upsettor*

**2.** What country was the 19th-century fossil hunter Mary Anning from?

**A)** England          **B)** USA          **C)** France

**3.** The Triassic, Jurassic and Cretaceous Periods are known as what era?

**A)** Cenozoic          **B)** Mesozoic          **C)** Paleozoic

**4.** The bony plates covering many armoured dinosaurs are called osteoderms. True or false?

**5.** The scientist who discovered the marine reptile *Elasmosaurus* reconstructed it incorrectly. Where did he place the head?

**A)** On its tail          **B)** On its foot          **C)** On its back

### QUESTIONS FOR KIDS

**1.** Which of these is a genuine dinosaur?

**A)** *Dumboraptor*     **B)** *Bambiraptor*     **C)** *Elsaraptor*

**2.** When dinosaurs emerged, all the land was combined into one supercontinent which we now call _____?

**A)** Pangaea          **B)** Megaland          **C)** Atlantis

**3.** What caused the dinosaurs to die out?

**A)** High winds          **B)** Tidal waves          **C)** An asteroid striking Earth

**4.** Some dinosaurs had two brains. True or false?

**5.** What is the name of the group of spikes on the tail of a stegosaur?

**A)** Spikemizer          **B)** Thagomizer          **C)** Pointemizer

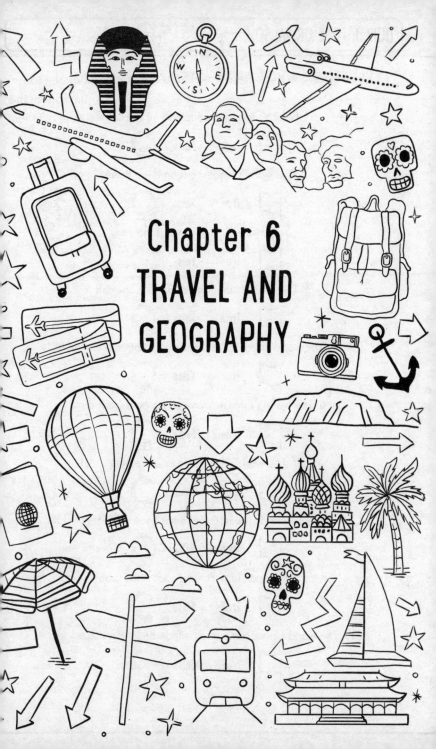

# Chapter 6
# TRAVEL AND
# GEOGRAPHY

Tick whether you think these travel facts are true or false.

1. New York is the capital city of the USA.

   True    False

2. The world's biggest ocean is the Pacific.

   True    False

3. The currency of Japan is the yen.

   True    False

4. The official language of Brazil is Spanish.

   True    False

5. The world's largest country by population is China.

   True    False

6. The world's largest country by area is Canada.

   True    False

7. The world's longest river is the Nile.

   True    False

8. The world's tallest mountain is Mount Everest.

   True    False

9. The world's largest hot desert is the Gobi.

   True    False

10. The world's longest mountain range on land is the Andes.

    True    False

For each of these questions, there is just one correct answer.
Circle the correct answer: A, B or C.

**1.** What percentage of the Earth's surface is covered in water?
A) 31%　　　　B) 51%　　　　C) 71%

**2.** What is the currency of France?
A) Franc　　　　B) Euro　　　　C) Dollar

**3.** Which was the first Disney theme park? It opened in 1955.
A) Disneyland　　　　B) Disney World　　　　C) Euro Disney

**4.** What sort of habitat is associated with the Amazon?
A) Grasslands　　　　B) Rainforest　　　　C) Desert

**5.** What is the capital of Australia?
A) Sydney　　　　B) Melbourne　　　　C) Canberra

**6.** Mount Etna is an active volcano in which European country?
A) Italy　　　　B) Germany　　　　C) Greece

**7.** What is the name of the 13th-century temple complex featured on the flag of Cambodia?
A) Machu Picchu　　　　B) Angkor Wat　　　　C) Taj Mahal

**8.** Fiji is a country made up of lots of islands in which ocean?
A) Atlantic　　　　B) Indian　　　　C) Pacific

**9.** Located in Venezuela, the world's tallest waterfall is _____?
A) Angel Falls　　　　B) Devil Falls　　　　C) Tall Falls

**10.** If you've just landed at John F. Kennedy International Airport, what country are you in?
A) Canada　　　　B) USA　　　　C) Ireland

There's something missing from each of these groups. Can you work out what it is? It's one of the options in the list at the side. Write your answers in the spaces provided.

Alaska
Antarctica
Argentina

**Group 1.** Which one is a continent?

North America      Europe          Asia

Africa             Australia       ...................

**Group 2.** Which one is an ocean?

Atlantic      Pacific

Indian        Arctic        ...................

Southern
Northern
Eastern

Nevada
Mississippi
Massachusetts

**Group 3.** Which one is a river?

Amazon        Yangtze

Nile          Congo        ...................

**Group 4.** Which one is a desert?

Sahara      Gobi

Mojave      Atacama      ...................

Halakari
Larahaki
Kalahari

A1
K2
Z3

**Group 5.** Which one is a mountain?

Everest        Kilimanjaro

Mont Blanc     Denali        ...................

Scandinavia
Suriname
Sweden

**Group 6.** Which one is a European country?

France      Greece

Denmark      Germany     ....................

**Group 7.** Which one is a Caribbean country?

Jamaica      Barbados

Dominica      Haiti     ....................

Mali
Cuba
Peru

Chad
Cyprus
Chile

**Group 8.** Which one is a South American country?

Brazil      Colombia

Venezeula      Uruguay     ....................

**Group 9.** Which one is an Asian country?

Japan      China

Malaysia      India     ....................

Thailand
Tonga
Peru

Laos
Latvia
Liberia

**Group 10.** Which one is an African country?

Algeria      Sudan

Botswana      Zambia     ....................

For each of these questions, there are two correct statements and one incorrect one. Can you work out which is which? Circle the one you think is a mistake.

### 1. CUNNING CAPITALS
A) The capital of France is Paris.
B) The capital of China is Beijing.
C) The capital of Brazil is Rio de Janeiro.

### 2. LANGUAGE LESSONS
A) The official language of India is Indian.
B) The official language of Spain is Spanish.
C) The official language of Germany is German.

### 3. CURRENCY AFFAIRS
A) The US dollar is the currency of the USA.
B) The Italian lira is the currency of Italy.
C) The Russian ruble is the currency of Russia.

### 4. SUPER SOUTHERNERS
A) South Africa is the southernmost country in Africa.
B) Mongolia is the southernmost country in Asia.
C) Chile is the southernmost country in South America.

### 5. SPORTING CHANCE
A) The first modern Olympic Games took place in Athens in 1896.
B) London is the only city to have hosted the games three times, in 1908, 1948 and 2012.
C) The 2016 Olympic Games were held in Antarctica.

## 6. ICY INTELLIGENCE

**A)** Most of the world's freshwater is frozen in glaciers and ice caps.

**B)** Lake Victoria in Africa is the world's largest frozen lake.

**C)** There's an ice hotel in Sweden which is built every winter and melts away each summer.

## 7. FIENDISH FOODS

**A)** Biltong is food from southern Africa made from dried meat.

**B)** Wurst is a food from Europe made from pickled cabbage.

**C)** Sushi is a food from Japan made from rice and raw fish.

## 8. URBAN UNDERSTANDING

**A)** Miami is a city in the USA.

**B)** Munich is a city in Germany.

**C)** Bangkok is a city in China.

## 9. MOUNTAIN MAYHEM

**A)** The Alps are a mountain range in Europe.

**B)** The Andes are a mountain range in Africa.

**C)** The Himalayas are a mountain range in Asia.

## 10. FUN FESTIVALS

**A)** In Spain, there's an annual festival called the Olivetina where people throw olives at each other.

**B)** In the UK, there's a cheese-rolling festival during which people chase a round of cheese down a hill.

**C)** In Thailand, there's an annual Monkey Buffet Festival where people lay on a banquet for local wild monkeys.

# QUIZ 5: FILL IN THE BLANKS

Can you write in the word, or words, that are missing from these statements? For each statement, the correct answer is one of the options in the box to the side.

1. The UK's currency is the British ....................

Pound Dollar
Franc Euro

Inferior Superior
Exterior Posterior

2. Lake .................... is the largest of the five North American 'Great Lakes'.

3. The Olympic Games are held every .................... years in a different city.

Two Three
Four Five

Europe Africa
Australia Asia

4. .................... is the world's most populous continent, home to around 60% of the global population.

5. The Trans- .................... Railway is the world's longest train service, stretching for 9,289 km (5,772 miles).

American European
Siberian Australian

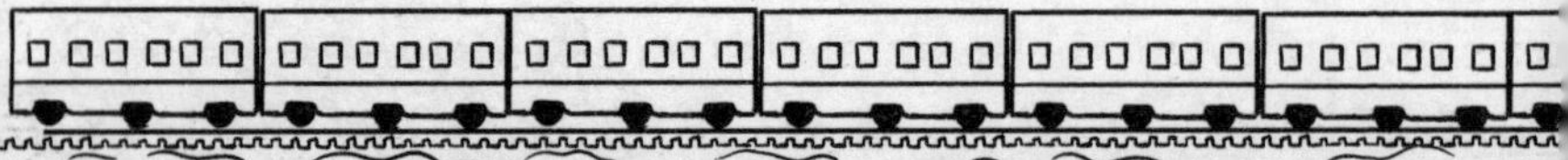

**6.** A .................... is a jet of hot water that shoots up out of a hole in the ground.

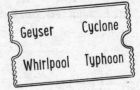

Geyser    Cyclone

Whirlpool    Typhoon

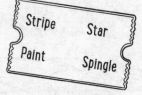

Stripe    Star

Paint    Spingle

**7.** The .................... -Spangled Banner is the national anthem of the USA.

**8.** In Australia, there is a .................... -shaped coral reef.

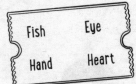

Fish    Eye

Hand    Heart

Russia    Monaco

Vatican City    Mexico

**9.** .................... is the world's smallest country, covering an area of just 0.49 sq km (0.2 sq miles)

**10.** Number .................... Downing Street is where the Prime Minister of the UK lives.

One    Five

Ten    1600

For this quiz, you need to work out which landmark is in which of the highlighted countries. Write your answers in the spaces.

**1. Tower Bridge**

COUNTRY ...............

**2. Statue of Christ the Redeemer**

COUNTRY

.................

**3. Tutankhamun's Tomb**

COUNTRY ...............

USA

BRAZIL

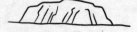

**4. Uluru**

COUNTRY ...............

**5. Mount Kilimanjaro**

COUNTRY ...............

7. Mount Rushmore

COUNTRY ................

6. Forbidden City

COUNTRY ................

8. The Parthenon

COUNTRY ................

UK

GREECE

RUSSIA

CHINA

SPAIN

EGYPT

TANZANIA

AUSTRALIA

9. Sagrada Familia

COUNTRY ................

10. St Basil's Cathedral

COUNTRY ................

Can you pick out the right answer from the two wrong ones in this multiple choice quiz?

**1.** What is the only continent with land in all four hemispheres: north, south, east and west?

**A)** Europe **B)** Asia **C)** Africa

**2.** The Great Barrier Reef lies off the coast of which country?

**A)** Australia **B)** Argentina **C)** Japan

**3.** Tunisia in Africa was used as a location for which series of films?

**A)** The Lord of the Rings **B)** Star Wars **C)** Harry Potter

**4.** What is the capital of Iceland?

**A)** Icetown **B)** Oslo **C)** Reykjavik

**5.** What are Japan's high-speed Shinkansen trains also known as?

**A)** Bullet trains **B)** Rocket trains **C)** Jet trains

**6.** 1600 Pennsylvania Avenue is the official address of which building?

**A)** Buckingham Palace **B)** The White House **C)** The Eiffel Tower

**7.** The Channel Tunnel links which two European countries?

**A)** Italy and Greece **B)** Spain and Ireland **C)** England and France

**8.** The explorer Roald Amundsen was the first person to reach where?

**A)** The South Pole **B)** The North Pole **C)** Bottom of the ocean

**9.** What is the nickname of the Boeing 747 plane?

**A)** Jumbo Jet **B)** Fat Flyer **C)** Heavy Hauler

**10.** What is the name of the festival celebrated each year in Mexico on 1–2 November?

**A)** Day of the Living **B)** Day of the Dead **C)** Day of the Zombies

Are these statements true or false? Tick your answers.

1. The Golden Gate Bridge in the USA is actually red.

   True    False

2. The capital of Turkey is Istanbul.

   True    False

3. Mexico City, the capital of Mexico, is sinking by over 30 cm (12 in) a year.

   True    False

4. The official language of the USA is English.

   True    False

5. The Oresund Bridge links the countries of Denmark and Sweden.

   True    False

6. The capital of Canada is Toronto.

   True    False

7. The Marianas Trench is the deepest place on the Earth's surface.

   True    False

8. Ecuador's Mount Chimborazo is closer to space than Mount Everest.

   True    False

9. The Hindu festival Diwali is also known as the 'Festival of Darkness'.

   True    False

10. The Amazon river holds more water than any other river on Earth.

   True    False

This is a game for two or more players. One reads out the clues, while the others try to work out what country is being talked about. Add up the points at the end – the player with the most is the winner.

**QUESTION 1.**
Clue 1 (4 points): By population, I'm the third largest country in the world.
Clue 2 (3 points): My capital city is not my largest city.
Clue 3 (2 points): I'm governed by a president.
Clue 4 (1 point): I'm made up of 50 states.

**QUESTION 2.**
Clue 1 (4 points): I'm a large Asian country.
Clue 2 (3 points): I occupy several islands. The largest is called Honshu.
Clue 3 (2 points): I'm known for electronics companies.
Clue 4 (1 point): My capital is Tokyo.

**QUESTION 3.**
Clue 1 (4 points): I'm a large country in South America.
Clue 2 (3 points): My football team has won the World Cup twice, in 1978 and 1986.
Clue 3 (2 points): In my centre are grasslands called *pampas*, where horse riders called *gauchos* rear cattle.
Clue 4 (1 point): My capital is Buenos Aires.

**QUESTION 4.**
Clue 1 (4 points): I'm a large Asian country.
Clue 2 (3 points): For thousands of years, I was ruled by emperors.
Clue 3 (2 points): I'm the only place where pandas live in the wild.
Clue 4 (1 point): My most famous feature is a long stone wall.

**QUESTION 5.**
Clue 1 (4 points): I'm a large country divided between Europe and Asia.
Clue 2 (3 points): I have large stretches of forest, home to bears and tigers.
Clue 3 (2 points): I was once a communist country.
Clue 4 (1 point): My capital is Moscow.

## QUESTION 6.
**Clue 1 (4 points)**: I'm a Western European nation.
**Clue 2 (3 points)**: I'm famous for my writers and musicians.
**Clue 3 (2 points)**: I'm made up of four different countries.
**Clue 4 (1 point)**: My capital is the home of Buckingham Palace.

## QUESTION 7.
**Clue 1 (4 points)**: I'm a Western European nation.
**Clue 2 (3 points)**: I'm famous for my food and fashions.
**Clue 3 (2 points)**: My southern coast is known as the Riviera.
**Clue 4 (1 point)**: My capital is home to the Eiffel Tower.

## QUESTION 8.
**Clue 1 (4 points)**: I'm an African country.
**Clue 2 (3 points)**: I'm home to lots of wildlife, including elephants
and lions.
**Clue 3 (2 points)**: Nelson Mandela used to be my president.
**Clue 4 (1 point)**: My largest cities include Cape Town and Johannesburg.

## QUESTION 9.
**Clue 1 (4 points)**: I'm a country in the Pacific Ocean.
**Clue 2 (3 points)**: I'm made up of several islands, including the North Island
and the South Island.
**Clue 3 (2 points)**: The original people of this land are known as Māori.
**Clue 4 (1 point)**: My capital is Wellington and my national bird is the kiwi.

## QUESTION 10.
**Clue 1 (4 points)**: I'm a country in south-east Europe.
**Clue 2 (3 points)**: I have a civilization that stretches back thousands
of years.
**Clue 3 (2 points)**: I'm famous for my philosophers and thinkers.
**Clue 4 (1 point)**: The people here used to worship
the gods of Mount Olympus, including Zeus,
Apollo and Aphrodite.

Let's see who's smarter, children or adults. The questions at the top are for adults, and should be asked by kids, while the questions down below are for kids, and should be asked by adults. You can ask them all at once or take it in turns.

### QUESTIONS FOR ADULTS

1. What is Japan's tallest mountain called?
**A)** Mount Fuji    **B)** Mount Muji    **C)** Mount Hugey

2. What is the capital of Indonesia?
**A)** Vientiane        **B)** Jakarta        **C)** Bali

3. The country of Equatorial Guinea is in which continent?
**A)** South America        **B)** Africa        **C)** Asia

4. Canada has more lakes than any other country. True or false?

5. What is the name of the line of latitude located at 23.5° north?
**A)** Tropic of Capricorn    **B)** Tropic of Cancer    **C)** Prime Meridian

### QUESTIONS FOR KIDS

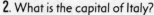

1. By what name are Australia's central areas
of desert known?
**A)** The Outback    **B)** The Backout    **C)** The Billabongs

2. What is the capital of Italy?
**A)** Milan        **B)** Rome        **C)** Naples

3. The country of Kazakhstan is on which continent?
**A)** Europe        **B)** Asia        **C)** South America

4. The Canadian flag has a red maple leaf at its centre. True or false?

5. What is the name of the imaginary line that runs horizontally around the centre of the Earth? Clue: it begins with 'E'.

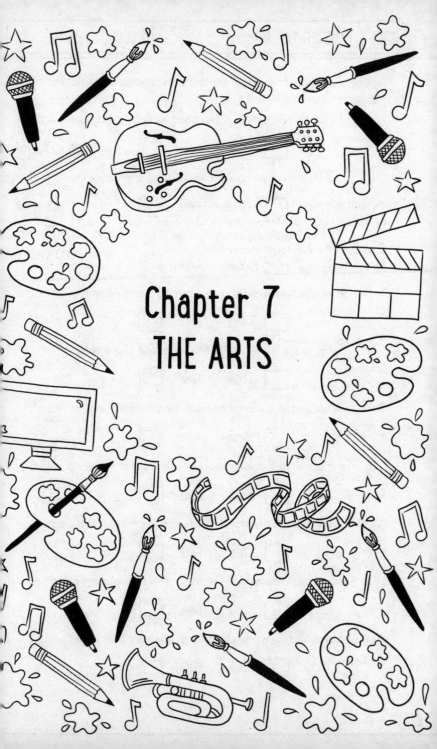

# Chapter 7
# THE ARTS

Tick whether you think these artistic facts are true or false.

1. The *Mona Lisa* was painted by Leonardo da Vinci.

   True   False

2. There are six novels in the Harry Potter series.

   True   False

3. The Louvre is an art museum in London, UK.

   True   False

4. Sir Christopher Robin was a famous British architect.

   True   False

5. The space ranger in *Toy Story* is called Buzz Blaster.

   True   False

6. Red, yellow and blue cannot be made by mixing any other colours.

   True   False

7. The American artist Jackson Pollock is famed for his lifelike sculptures.

   True   False

8. The Spanish artist Salvador Dalí is famous for his surreal pictures.

   True   False

9. The French artist Claude Monet is famous for his sunflower paintings.

   True   False

10. If a book or film form part of a trilogy, there are three other parts.

   True   False

For each of these questions, there is just one correct answer.
Circle the correct answer: A, B or C.

**1.** The world's largest annual arts festival is held in which city?
A) Edinburgh, Scotland    B) New York, USA    C) Beijing, China

**2.** The earliest known sculptures were made of what material?
A) Glass              B) Stone              C) Plastic

**3.** Frida Kahlo was a 20th-century artist from which country?
A) Spain              B) Japan              C) Mexico

**4.** What type of dance shoes have metal plates on the heel and toe?
A) Ballet             B) Tap                C) Ballroom

**5.** In a famous picture by Botticelli, Venus is shown standing on a _____?
A) Boat               B) Cloud              C) Shell

**6.** What sort of stories is the ancient Greek writer Aesop best known for?
A) Fables             B) Novels             C) Whodunnits

**7.** The protective edge around the edge of a painting is called the _____?
A) Frame              B) Canvas             C) Hook

**8.** What is the magical land in *The Lion, the Witch and the Wardrobe*?
A) Neverland          B) Oz                 C) Narnia

**9.** What name is given to a piece of art made by sticking together
different pieces of material?
A) Tapestry           B) Collage            C) Oil painting

**10.** Authors used to write with feather pens called _____?
A) Frills             B) Quills             C) Drills

In each of these lists, there's something that doesn't belong.
Can you spot what it is? Circle your answers.

1. Can you work out which one of these people is the singer hiding
among the painters?

Holbein            Manet              Madonna

Rubens             Raphael

2. Which of these is not a character from *The Lord of the Rings*?

Bilbo              Gandalf            Sauron

Paddington         Gollum

3. Which of these is not a material usually used to make sculptures?

Stone              Clay               Wood

Plastic            Feathers

4. Which of these would an artist not normally have in their toolkit?

Spanner            Palette            Brush

Charcoal           Eraser

5. Can you spot the film director in among the poets?

Emily Dickinson    Steven Spielberg   Maya Angelou

John Keats         Christina Rossetti

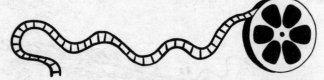

**6.** Which of these is not one of the main characters in a novel by Charles Dickens?

Billy Bomblefool          David Copperfield          Nicholas Nickleby

Oliver Twist          Pip


**7.** Which of these is not a genuine art movement?

Art Nouveau          Art Deco          Impersonationism

Expressionism          Minimalism


**8.** Which of these is not a main character in a Roald Dahl book?

Matilda          Max          Danny

James          George


**9.** Which of these is not a genuine style of architecture?

Doric          Ionic          Corinthian

Baroque          Haute couture


**10.** Which of these is not a play by the most famous English writer of all time, William Shakespeare?

*Hamlet*          *Macbeth*          *Othello*

*Peter Pan*          *Twelfth Night*

For each of these questions, there are two correct statements and one incorrect one. Can you work out which is which? Circle the one you think is a mistake.

### 1. AUTHORIAL ANSWERS
**A)** *Pig Heart Boy* was written by Malorie Blackman.
**B)** *Pippi Longstocking* was written by Astrid Lindgren.
**C)** *The Gruffalo* was written by Dr. Seuss.

### 2. HARRY UP AND DECIDE
**A)** Harry Potter studies at Hogwarts School.
**B)** He belongs to Slytherin house.
**C)** His closest friends at school are Hermione and Ron.

### 3. COLOUR CONUNDRUM
**A)** If you mix yellow and red, you get orange.
**B)** If you mix blue and red, you get purple.
**C)** If you mix blue and pink, you get green.

### 4. MICHELANGELO'S MYSTERIES
**A)** The artist Michelangelo was born in Sweden.
**B)** He spent four years painting the ceiling of the Sistine Chapel in Rome.
**C)** His most famous statue is of the Biblical king, David.

### 5. MULLING MUSEUMS
**A)** The National Gallery is an art museum in London, UK.
**B)** The Rijksmuseum is an art museum in New York, USA.
**C)** The Uffizi is an art museum in Florence, Italy.

## 6. PHOTO PROBLEMS
**A)** The part of the camera you look through is called the viewfinder.

**B)** The button you press to take a photograph is called the lens.

**C)** The hole that lets light into a camera is called the aperture.

## 7. CARTOON CHOICES
**A)** *Tangled*'s main character is called Cinderella.

**B)** *The Lion King*'s main character is called Simba.

**C)** *Frozen*'s main character is called Elsa.

## 8. RE-EXAMINING THE RENAISSANCE
**A)** The Renaissance was a European cultural and societal movement between the 14th and 17th centuries.

**B)** The word 'Renaissance' means 'excellent paintings'.

**C)** The Renaissance started in Italy.

## 9. SUPER SUPPOSITIONS
**A)** The secret identity of the superhero Batman is Bruce Banner.

**B)** The secret identity of the superhero Superman is Clark Kent.

**C)** The secret identity of the superhero Spiderman is Peter Parker.

## 10. PERFORMANCE PUZZLES
**A)** The Bolshoi is a ballet theatre in Moscow, Russia.

**B)** La Scala is an opera house in Milan, Italy.

**C)** Carnegie Hall is a concert venue in London, UK.

Can you write in the word, or words, that are missing from these statements? For each statement, the correct answer is one of the options written in the box.

1. Frank Lloyd Wright, Zaha Hadid and Le Corbusier were all famous ..................

Painters

Dancers

Singers

Architects

Smithsonian     Prado

Musée d'Orsay     Tate

2. The ............... in Madrid is Spain's largest art museum.

3. *The Son of Man* is a painting by the Belgian artist René Magritte, showing a man in a suit with an ............... in front of his face.

Apple     Orange

Insect     Aardvark

Cartoon     Conceptual

Graffiti     Oil

4. ............... pictures are ones that have been painted onto public walls, often without permission.

5. In *The Wizard of Oz*, Dorothy, the ............... the Tin Man and the Cowardly Lion travel together to the Emerald City.

Munchkin

Glinda

Wicked Witch

Scarecrow

**6.** *Girl with a* ................. *Earring* is a famous picture by the Dutch painter Vermeer.

Silver     Pearl

Diamond     Gold

Action!     Do it!

Act now!     Talk!

**7.** A movie director shouts ................. to start filming a scene.

**8.** A movie director then shouts ................. to stop filming a scene.

End!     Stop it!

Cut!     Halt!

Chocolates     Candles

Ice cubes     Clocks

**9.** Melting ................. feature in the painting *The Persistence of Memory* by the Spanish artist Salvador Dali.

**10.** The popular film, ................. *Dalmatians*, is based on a book by the British author Dodie Smith.

1     11

101     1,001

Can you identify all of these items of art equipment from the list below? Write your answers in the spaces.

> **ART EQUIPMENT**
>
> Easel                    Mechanical Pencil
>
> Oil paints               Eraser
>
> Watercolour paints       Airbrush
>
> Palette                  Canvas
>
> Palette knife            Paintbrush

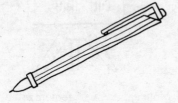

ITEM 1. ......................

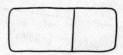

ITEM 2. ......................

ITEM 3. ......................

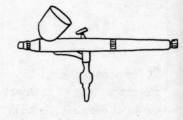

ITEM 4. ......................

ITEM 5. ........................

ITEM 6. ........................

ITEM 7. ........................

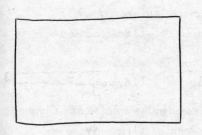

ITEM 8. ........................

ITEM 9. ........................

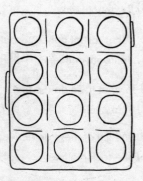

ITEM 10. ........................

Can you pick out the right answer from the two wrong ones in this multiple choice quiz?

**1.** In the 19th century, the French artist Edgar Degas created a famous sculpture known as the *Little* _____?

**A)** *Learner*          **B)** *Dancer*          **C)** *Juggler*

**2.** The earliest known cave paintings are pictures of what?

**A)** Animals          **B)** Cars          **C)** Buildings

**3.** Eric Carle wrote a book called *The Very Hungry* _____?

**A)** *Elephant*          **B)** *Caterpillar*          **C)** *Hippopotamus*

**4.** The *Mona Lisa* is famous for her mysterious _____?

**A)** Nose          **B)** Feet          **C)** Smile

**5.** What material are the statues in the UK's Madame Tussaud's made from?

**A)** Stone          **B)** Wax          **C)** Clay

**6.** What is the name of the dragon in *The Hobbit*?

**A)** Smaug          **B)** Borg          **C)** Godzilla

**7.** The art style where pictures are created using lots of geometric shapes is known as?

**A)** Rectangulism          **B)** Triangulism          **C)** Cubism

**8.** What sort of dancers would be most likely to wear a tutu?

**A)** Ballroom dancers          **B)** Folk dancers          **C)** Ballet dancers

**9.** In what town do the titular family from *The Simpsons* live?

**A)** Springfield          **B)** Toontown          **C)** Bedrock

**10.** Which of these detectives was created by the writer Agatha Christie?

**A)** Sherlock Holmes          **B)** Hercule Poirot          **C)** Hazel Wong

Are these statements true or false? Tick your answers.

1. The Teenage Mutant Ninja Turtles are named after Italian artists.

True    False

2. *The Phantom of the Cinema* is a famous stage musical.

True    False

3. Winnie the Pooh had a lion friend called Leo.

True    False

4. One of Andy Warhol's most famous pictures is of soup cans.

True    False

5. Tempera is a type of paint made with cheese.

True    False

6. The main character in the His Dark Materials trilogy is called Lyra.

True    False

7. The art term Impressionism was originally used as an insult.

True    False

8. The artist known as 'El Greco' (the Greek) was actually from Spain.

True    False

9. The character Paddington Bear is from Mexico.

True    False

10. Pointillism is a technique for creating pictures using tiny dots.

True    False

This is a game for two or more players. One reads out the clues, while the others try to work out who is being talked about. The answer is either an artist, a writer or a singer.

**QUESTION 1.**
**Clue 1 (4 points):** I was born in Italy in 1452.
**Clue 2 (3 points):** I was one of the major figures of the Renaissance.
**Clue 3 (2 points):** I was both an artist and an inventor.
**Clue 4 (1 point):** One of my most famous paintings is *The Last Supper*.

**QUESTION 2.**
**Clue 1 (4 points):** I was born in the USA in 1981.
**Clue 2 (3 points):** I was singer in the group Destiny's Child.
**Clue 3 (2 points):** I am also one of the best-selling solo artists of all time.
**Clue 4 (1 point):** In 2008, I married the rapper, Jay-Z.

**QUESTION 3.**
**Clue 1 (4 points):** I was born in England in 1564.
**Clue 2 (3 points):** I grew up to become an actor and playwright.
**Clue 3 (2 points):** I'm sometimes called the 'Bard of Avon'.
**Clue 4 (1 point):** Some of my most famous works include *A Midsummer Night's Dream*, *Romeo and Juliet* and *King Lear*.

**QUESTION 4.**
**Clue 1 (4 points):** I was born in the Netherlands in 1853.
**Clue 2 (3 points):** I produced over 2,000 paintings.
**Clue 3 (2 points):** My paintings are now some of the most expensive pieces of art in the world, but I only sold one in my lifetime.
**Clue 4 (1 point):** My works include several paintings of sunflowers.

**QUESTION 5.**
**Clue 1 (4 points):** I was born in 1875 in Denmark.
**Clue 2 (3 points):** I wrote many fairy tales.
**Clue 3 (2 points):** Many of my stories have been turned into films.
**Clue 4 (1 point):** My most famous works include *The Little Mermaid*, *The Ugly Duckling* and *The Emperor's New Clothes*.

## QUESTION 6.

**Clue 1 (4 points):** I was born in the USA in 1977.

**Clue 2 (3 points):** I'm a famous rapper, musician and fashion designer.

**Clue 3 (2 points):** In 2020, I ran unsuccessfully for US president.

**Clue 4 (1 point):** In 2014, I married the reality TV star Kim Kardashian.

## QUESTION 7.

**Clue 1 (4 points):** I was born in Germany in 1770.

**Clue 2 (3 points):** I grew up to become a composer.

**Clue 3 (2 points):** I lost my hearing as I got older but I still carried on composing music.

**Clue 4 (1 point):** My most famous works include *Moonlight Sonata* and my Fifth Symphony.

## QUESTION 8.

**Clue 1 (4 points):** I was born in England in 1866.

**Clue 2 (3 points):** I was a writer and illustrator.

**Clue 3 (2 points):** I wrote 23 books for children featuring animal stories.

**Clue 4 (1 point):** My books include the characters Peter Rabbit, Squirrel Nutkin and Mrs Tiggy-Winkle.

## QUESTION 9.

**Clue 1 (4 points):** I was born in England in 1965.

**Clue 2 (3 points):** I write books both using my own name and the name Robert Galbraith.

**Clue 3 (2 points):** I'm a best-selling author of the 21st century.

**Clue 4 (1 point):** My most famous creation is Harry Potter.

## QUESTION 10.

**Clue 1 (4 points):** I was born in the USA in 1989.

**Clue 2 (3 points):** I'm one of the best-selling singers of all time.

**Clue 3 (2 points):** My last name means 'fast'.

**Clue 4 (1 point):** Some of my most famous songs include 'Shake it Off', 'Look What You Made Me Do' and 'Cardigan'.

Let's see who's smarter, children or adults. The questions at the top are for adults, and should be asked by kids, while the questions down below are for kids, and should be asked by adults. You can ask them all at once or take it in turns.

## QUESTIONS FOR ADULTS

1. What is the award for the best film at the Cannes Film Festival?
**A)** Golden Bear   **B)** Palme d'Or   **C)** Golden Globe

2. The Japanese artist Hokusai is famous for his painting *The Great _____*?
**A)** *Wave*          **B)** *Cloud*          **C)** *White Shark*

3. How many lines are there in a sonnet?
**A)** 13          **B)** 14          **C)** 15

4. The artist and director Steve McQueen is from the USA. True or false?

5. Which British artist painted *A Bigger Splash*?
**A)** Damien Hirst     **B)** Tracey Emin     **C)** David Hockney

## QUESTIONS FOR KIDS

1. What awards are given out at the Academy Awards?
**A)** Emmys          **B)** Oscars          **C)** Baftas

2. The Norwegian painter Edvard Munch is famous for his painting *The _____*?
**A)** *Scream*          **B)** *Yell*          **C)** *Shout*

3. How many lines are there in a limerick?
**A)** Four          **B)** Five          **C)** Six

4. The painter Francisco Goya was from Portugal. True or False?

5. Geoffrey Chaucer wrote the *_____ Tales*?
**A)** *New York*          **B)** *Oxford*          **C)** *Canterbury*

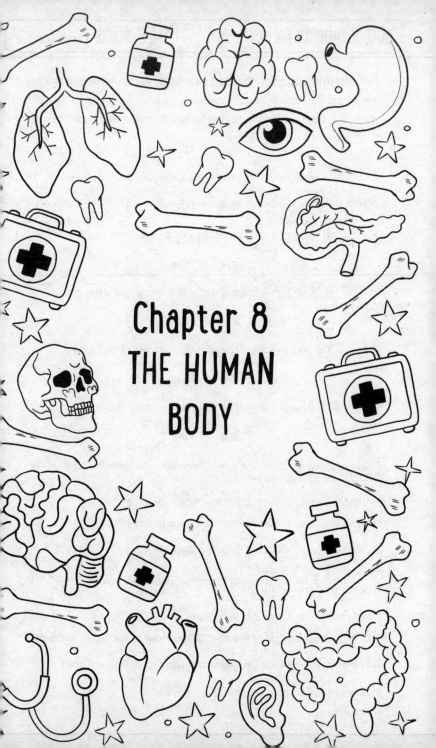

# Chapter 8
# THE HUMAN BODY

Tick whether you think these human body facts are true or false.

1. The study of the human body is known as anatomy.

   True    False

2. The blood inside your body is actually blue, not red.

   True    False

3. The skin is the heaviest organ of the human body.

   True    False

4. Your 'funny' bone is actually a nerve, not a bone.

   True    False

5. Adults have more bones in their bodies than children.

   True    False

6. The heart controls all the other organs in your body.

   True    False

7. Our eyes see things upside down; the brain turns them the right way up.

   True    False

8. Some babies are born with teeth.

   True    False

9. Blue is the most common human eye colour.

   True    False

10. More than half of all the body's bones are in the hands and feet.

   True    False

For each of these questions, there is just one correct answer.
Circle the correct answer: A, B or C.

1. A cardiac doctor deals with which part of the body?
A) Heart          B) Lungs          C) Feet

2. Along with the tongue, what body part helps you to taste things?
A) Eyes          B) Ears          C) Nose

3. What is the name of the hard substance that covers your teeth?
A) Dentine          B) Enamel          C) Bone

4. What is the name of the spongy tissue inside bones?
A) Marrow          B) Courgette          C) Zucchini

5. What substance is produced by the mouth to help break down food?
A) Mucus          B) Bile          C) Saliva

6. What body parts connect muscles to bones?
A) Nails          B) Tendons          C) Capillaries

7. What is the strongest muscle in the human body?
A) Biceps (arm)          B) Masseter (jaw)          C) Gluteus Maximus (buttocks)

8. On average, how much blood is in an adult human body?
A) 1 litre          B) 5 litres          C) 10 litres

9. Which of these is not part of the digestive system?
A) Ears          B) Mouth          C) Stomach

10. At what age does the human body grow quickest?
A) 0–2 years old     B) 12–14 years old     C) 18–21 years old

In each of these lists, there's something that doesn't belong.
Can you work out what it is? Circle your answers.

1. Do you know which one of these isn't part of the eye?

Iris              Cornea              Pupil

Pancreas          Lens

2. Which of these is not a type of joint in the body?

Hinge             Ball and socket     Gliding

Pivot             Pulmonary

3. Which of these would you not find in a cell?

Wall              Nucleus             Membrane

Vertebra          Cytoplasm

4. Which of these is not a genuine body system?

Respiratory       Circulatory         Electric

Digestive         Immune

5. Can you pick out the bone from among the teeth?

Tibia             Incisor             Canine

Premolar          Molar

**6**. Which of these is not part of the ear?

Drum          Stick          Lobe

Canal         Cochlea

**7**. Which of these does not form part of the nervous system?

Brain         Kidneys        Spinal cord

Sensory organs   Nerves

**8**. Can you pick out the organ from among the bones?

Mandible      Clavicle       Rib

Sternum       Spleen

**9**. Can you pick out the muscle from among the hormones?

Triceps       Insulin        Adrenalin

Dopamine      Histamine

**10**. Which of these terms does not relate to hair?

Follicle      Root           Lid

Shaft         Sebaceous gland

For each of these questions, there are two correct statements and one incorrect one. Can you work out which is which? Circle the one you think is a mistake.

## 1. LUNG LESSONS

**A)** The average person takes around 25,000 breaths a day.

**B)** The lungs take in carbon dioxide and expel oxygen.

**C)** To make room for the heart, the left lung is smaller than the right lung.

## 2. MUCH ADO ABOUT MUCUS

**A)** Mucus helps keep dust and bacteria out of our mouths and noses.

**B)** An average person produces around a litre of mucus a day.

**C)** Mucus is always green.

## 3. DENTAL DECIDERS

**A)** Teeth keep growing, and replacing themselves, throughout our lives.

**B)** By adulthood, most people have 32 teeth.

**C)** Around two thirds of each tooth is hidden from view in our gums.

## 4. SKULL SECRETS

**A)** The scientific name for the skull is the cranium.

**B)** Newborn babies have holes in their skulls known as fontanelles.

**C)** The skull is made of the hardest substance in the human body.

## 5. BACKBONE BREAKDOWN

**A)** The spine is made up of lots of small bones called vertebrae.

**B)** Humans and giraffes have the same number of vertebrae in their neck: seven.

**C)** There are no muscles in the spine, just bones and tendons.

## 6. A LOOK AT LOCKS

**A)** The hair on your head grows around 3 cm (1 in) a year.

**B)** Humans have hair everywhere on their bodies except for their palms, the soles of their feet and their lips.

**C)** Hair is made of keratin, the same substance as your nails.

## 7. PROTECTIVE PUZZLES

**A)** Eyebrows stop sweat from getting in your eyes.

**B)** Eardrums stop small particles from getting in your ears.

**C)** Eyelashes stop sweat and small particles from getting in your mouth.

## 8. RIBBING REVISION

**A)** Men have fewer ribs than women.

**B)** All ribs are attached to the spine.

**C)** The ribs form a protective cage around the heart and lungs.

## 9. PAIRS OF POSERS

**A)** Most people have two kidneys.

**B)** Most people have two lungs.

**C)** Most people have two livers.

## 10. TASTY TESTERS

**A)** The average person is born with around 10,000 tastebuds.

**B)** The number of tastebuds decreases as you get older.

**C)** Tastebuds are arranged in groups on your tongue, which can sense different tastes, such as salty or sweet.

Can you write in the word, or words, that are missing from these statements? For each statement, the correct answer is one of the options written in the box at the side.

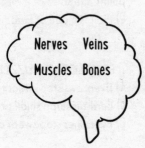

Nerves  Veins
Muscles  Bones

1. The brain sends messages along ................. to different parts of body, telling them what to do.

Veins            Arteries

Capillaries      Airways

2. ................. carry blood away from the heart.

3. You lose between ................. hairs from your head every day.

0-25          25-50

50-100        100-200

Clavicle (collar bone)

Sternum (breast bone)

Humerus (upper arm bone)

Femur (thigh bone)

4. The ................. is the longest bone in the body.

6 kph (3.7mph)

60 kph (37 mph)

160 kph (99 mph)

600 kph (373 mph)

5. When you sneeze, air (and snot) can leave your nose at up to .................

**6**. Your heart beats around ................ times a day.

> 1,000   10,000
>
> 100,000   1 million

> Melanin   Adrenalin
>
> Plasma   Blood

**7**. ................ is the substance that gives skin, hair and eyes their colour.

> Dinner plate
> Dining table
> Tennis court
> Football pitch

**8**. If laid out flat, our lungs would cover an area the size of a ................ .

**9**. Your fingernails grow around ................ mm a month.

> 0.35   3.5
>
> 35   350

**10**. The ................ is a long muscular tube that moves food from your mouth down into your stomach.

> Trachea   Duodenum
>
> Intestine   Oesophagus

Can you identify these body parts from their pictures? Write your answers in the spaces provided.

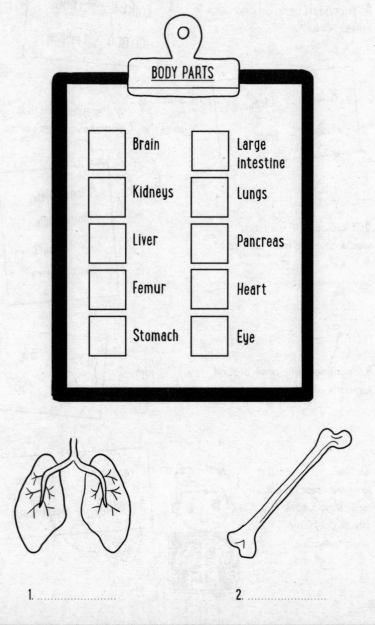

**BODY PARTS**

| | |
|---|---|
| ☐ Brain | ☐ Large intestine |
| ☐ Kidneys | ☐ Lungs |
| ☐ Liver | ☐ Pancreas |
| ☐ Femur | ☐ Heart |
| ☐ Stomach | ☐ Eye |

1. ..................

2. ..................

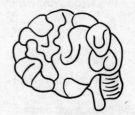

3. ......................

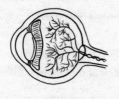

4. ......................

5. ......................

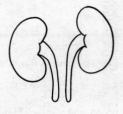

6. ......................

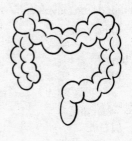

7. ......................

8. ......................

9. ......................

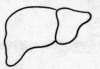

10. ......................

Can you pick out the right answer from the two wrong ones in this multiple choice quiz?

**1.** Hamstrings are large muscles located where in the body?
**A)** Back of the thighs    **B)** Front of the calves    **C)** Bottom of the feet

**2.** What system is responsible for moving blood through our bodies?
**A)** Respiratory      **B)** Circulatory      **C)** Digestive

**3.** The humerus (upper arm bone) is attached to the shoulder by what sort of joint?
**A)** Hinge      **B)** Gliding      **C)** Ball and socket

**4.** The smallest bone in the human body is found where?
**A)** Foot      **B)** Hand      **C)** Ear

**5.** What body parts connect bones to other bones?
**A)** Tonsils      **B)** Ligaments      **C)** Intestines

**6.** What is the name of an automatic reaction that doesn't involve the brain?
**A)** Redo      **B)** Reflex      **C)** Retrace

**7.** How much of the body's blood goes to the brain?
**A)** 1%      **B)** 10%      **C)** 20%

**8.** What part of the eye lets in light?
**A)** Pupil      **B)** Iris      **C)** Lens

**9.** The chemical that contains our genetic instructions is known by what three-letter code?
**A)** USD      **B)** LOL      **C)** DNA

**10.** Where in the body are new blood cells produced?
**A)** In bones      **B)** In the heart      **C)** In the mouth

Are these statements true or false? Tick your answers.

1. Your ears help you to balance.

True     False

2. The small intestine is actually longer than the large intestine.

True     False

3. An adult brain weighs around 10 kg (2.2 lbs).

True     False

4. You have more teeth as a child than you do as an adult.

True     False

5. You can swallow your own tongue.

True     False

6. There are four basic senses: touch, sight, hearing and smell.

True     False

7. The outer layer of skin is called the epidermis.

True     False

8. In the eye, the cells that can detect colours are called cones.

True     False

9. The voice box is also known as the larynx.

True     False

10. You absorb more oxygen through your skin than through your lungs.

True     False

This is a game for two or more players. One reads out the clues, while the others try to work out what is being talked about. The answer to every question is a body part (or parts).

**QUESTION 1.**
Clue 1 (4 points): I take up most of your body but you can't see me.
Clue 2 (3 points): I have lots of different parts.
Clue 3 (2 points): I help to support the body.
Clue 4 (1 point): I'm made up of bones.

**QUESTION 2.**
Clue 1 (4 points): There are two of me.
Clue 2 (3 points): I'm constantly changing size.
Clue 3 (2 points): I'm connected to your mouth.
Clue 4 (1 point): I'm responsible for breathing.

**QUESTION 3.**
Clue 1 (4 points): There are two of me.
Clue 2 (3 points): I form part of the head.
Clue 3 (2 points): I'm separated by something called a septum.
Clue 4 (1 point): I do all your smelling.

**QUESTION 4.**
Clue 1 (4 points): Sometimes I'm inside the body and sometimes I'm outside.
Clue 2 (3 points): I'm usually quite moist.
Clue 3 (2 points): I'm very flexible.
Clue 4 (1 point): I have very good taste.

**QUESTION 5.**
Clue 1 (4 points): I'm an organ.
Clue 2 (3 points): I sit in the abdomen on the right-hand side.
Clue 3 (2 points): I filter blood and help break down fats.
Clue 4 (1 point): I'm the only organ that can repair itself if I get damaged.

## QUESTION 6.
**Clue 1 (4 points):** I'm an organ.
**Clue 2 (3 points):** I'm protected by a hard case.
**Clue 3 (2 points):** I'm made up of several parts, including the cerebellum and the hypothalamus.
**Clue 4 (1 point):** I do all your thinking.

## QUESTION 7.
**Clue 1 (4 points):** I stick out from the body.
**Clue 2 (3 points):** I can bend and straighten.
**Clue 3 (2 points):** I'm part of the hand.
**Clue 4 (1 point):** I sit opposite the fingers.

## QUESTION 8.
**Clue 1 (4 points):** I'm an organ.
**Clue 2 (3 points):** I'm mainly made of muscle.
**Clue 3 (2 points):** I keep the beat.
**Clue 4 (1 point):** I pump blood around the body.

## QUESTION 9.
**Clue 1 (4 points):** I'm a bone.
**Clue 2 (3 points):** I protect other bones.
**Clue 3 (2 points):** My scientific name is 'patella'.
**Clue 4 (1 point):** I sit in the middle of the leg, about halfway up.

## QUESTION 10.
**Clue 1 (4 points):** There are two of me.
**Clue 2 (3 points):** I'm partly inside the body and partly outside.
**Clue 3 (2 points):** The outside part is quite fleshy while the inside part is made up of lots of little bones and muscles.
**Clue 4 (1 point):** I do all your hearing.

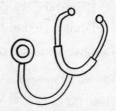

Let's see who's smarter, children or adults. The questions at the top are for adults, and should be asked by kids, while the questions down below are for kids, and should be asked by adults. You can ask them all at once or take it in turns.

## QUESTIONS FOR ADULTS

1. What body part does food enter when it leaves the stomach?

A) Small intestine    B) Large intestine    C) Oesophagus

2. What is the name of the substance produced by the liver that helps break down fats?

A) Bile    B) Mucus    C) Chyme

3. What sort of doctor specialises in children's illnesses?

A) Pathologist    B) Paediatrician    C) Podiatrist

4. The disease rickets is caused by a lack of vitamin D. True or false?

5. There are three types of muscle: skeletal, smooth and _____?

A) Pulmonary    B) Digestive    C) Cardiac

## QUESTIONS FOR KIDS

1. The process of digestion starts where in the body?

A) Mouth    B) Oesophagus    C) Stomach

2. What is the name of the light-sensitive layer of tissue at the back of the eye that transmits visual signals to the brain?

A) Retina    B) Appendix    C) Diaphragm

3. A dermatologist is a doctor that deals with which part of the body?

A) Feet    B) Skin    C) Eyes

4. The disease scurvy is caused by a lack of vitamin C. True or false?

5. There are three types of blood vessel: arteries, veins and _____?

A) Adenonids    B) Neurons    C) Capillaries

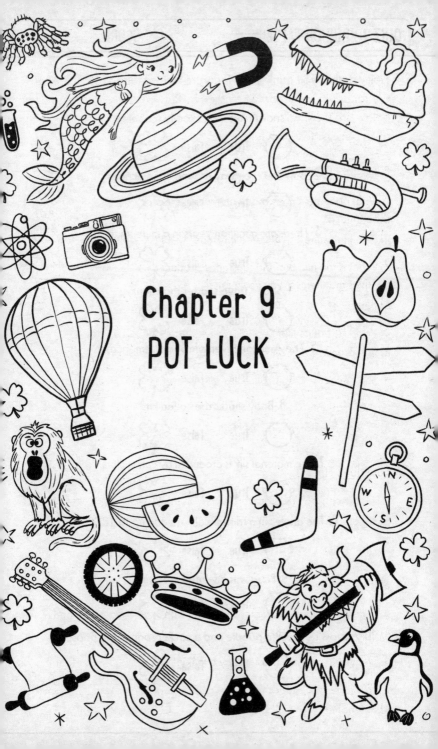

# Chapter 9
# POT LUCK

Tick whether you think these facts are true or false.

1. All snowflakes look exactly the same.

    True    False

2. Bats find their way around using echoes.

    True    False

3. There are a million years in a millennium.

    True    False

4. Sound travels faster than light.

    True    False

5. The Amazon River is in South America.

    True    False

6. Baby sharks are called kits.

    True    False

7. The material silk is produced by caterpillars.

    True    False

8. The angles in a triangle always add up to 180°.

    True    False

9. Pizza was invented in Spain.

    True    False

10. A cross between a poodle and a cocker spaniel is a poospan.

    True    False

For each of these questions, there is just one correct answer.
Circle the correct answer: A, B or C.

**1.** Diego Maradona was famous for playing which sport?

**A)** Football      **B)** Baseball      **C)** Tennis

**2.** What is the name of the ape-like monster said to live in the forests of North America?

**A)** Big Head      **B)** Big Foot      **C)** Big Hand

**3.** Roughly how far is the Earth from the Sun?

**A)** 149,000 km (92,600 miles)

**B)** 14.9 million km (9.2 million miles)

**C)** 149 million km (92 million miles)

**4.** What is the name of the kingdom in the film *Frozen*?

**A)** Narnia      **B)** Arendelle      **C)** Middle Earth

**5.** Lima is the capital of which South American country?

**A)** Peru      **B)** Brazil      **C)** Argentina

**6.** Who was President of the USA just before Joe Biden?

**A)** Barack Obama      **B)** George W. Bush      **C)** Donald Trump

**7.** The molten rock that flows out of a volcano is known as _____?

**A)** Magma      **B)** Lava      **C)** Ash

**8.** The Olympic Games originated in which country?

**A)** USA      **B)** France      **C)** Greece

**9.** What is the currency of Australia?

**A)** Australian pound      **B)** Australian euro      **C)** Australian dollar

**10.** Roughly how many species of monkey are there?

**A)** Around 26      **B)** Around 260      **C)** Around 2,600

In each of these lists, there's something that doesn't belong.
Can you work out what it is? Circle your answers.

1. Can you spot the reptile hiding among the amphibians?

Frog                    Toad                    Newt

Salamander              Turtle

2. Which of these items of clothing would someone from ancient Rome
not have worn?

Tunic                   Sandals                 Brooch

Waistcoat               Toga

3. Which of the following isn't a genuine US baseball team?

Miami Black Sox         Boston Red Sox          Detroit Tigers

Los Angeles Angels      New York Yankees

4. Can you pick out the tree from the flowers?

Rose                    Spruce                  Iris

Daisy                   Orchid

5. Which of the following isn't a real type of whale?

Bowhead                 Humpback                Blubber

Beluga                  Narwhal

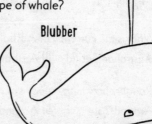

**6.** Can you pick out the brass instrument from this woodwind section?

Oboe          Clarinet          Flute

Trombone      Bassoon

**7.** Can you find the African country among the South American ones?

Brazil        Argentina         Kenya

Colombia      Chile

**8.** Which of the following isn't an online social media company?

Facebook      Wikipedia         Twitter

Instagram     Pinterest

**9.** Which of these stories isn't a traditional fairy tale?

*Snow White*      *Cinderella*          *Hansel and Gretel*

*The Goat Prince*   *Beauty and the Beast*

**10.** All these animals are cats, apart from one. Can you find it?

Lynx          Caracal           Margay

Snow leopard  Coyote

For each of these questions, there are two correct statements and one incorrect one. Can you work out which is which? Circle the one you think is a mistake.

## 1. IDENTITY PARADE
A) Identical twins have the same hair colour.
B) Identical twins have the same eye colour.
C) Identical twins have the same fingerprints.

## 2. A GERM OF AN IDEA
A) One of Earth's newest life forms, bacteria, have only been around for about 200 years.
B) There are more bacteria in your mouth than there are people in Asia.
C) Many bacteria are used for making foods, such as cheeses, pickles and yoghurts.

## 3. NAMING NOTIONS
A) The Rubik's Cube was invented by Erno Rubik.
B) The light bulb was invented by Laura Light.
C) The saxophone was invented by Adolphe Sax.

## 4. PRESIDENTIAL PROBLEMS
A) The US president lives in the White House.
B) US presidential elections are held every five years.
C) The partner of the US president is known as the First Lady (or First Gentleman).

## 5. MULLING MOUNTAINS
A) Mont Blanc is a mountain in Europe.
B) Everest is a mountain in Africa.
C) Denali is a mountain in North America.

## 6. HEADMASTERS
**A)** The Egyptian god, Ra, had the head of a giraffe.

**B)** The Egyptian god, Sobek, had the head of a crocodile.

**C)** The Egyptian god, Bast, had the head of a cat.

## 7. LESSONS IN LAND
**A)** An area of land surrounded by sea on two sides is a seamount.

**B)** An area of land surrounded by sea on three sides is a peninsula.

**C)** An area of land surrounded by sea on all sides is an island.

## 8. GUESSING THE GAME
**A)** Brazil have won the men's football World Cup five times.

**B)** Brazil have won the women's football World Cup six times.

**C)** Brazil's football teams usually play in yellow tops.

## 9. HAIRY HIGHLIGHTS
**A)** Adult humans have about a tenth of the number of hairs on their body as adult chimpanzees.

**B)** The sea otter has more hair on its body than any other animal.

**C)** A tiger's skin has the same pattern of stripes as its fur.

## 10. MYTHICAL MEMORY TEST
**A)** A mythical creature that is half human and half fish is a mermaid.

**B)** A mythical creature that is half human and half bull is a toreador.

**C)** A mythical creature that is half human and half horse is a centaur.

Can you write in the word, or words, that are missing from these statements? For each statement, the correct answer is one of the options written in the box at the side.

1. Unlike monkeys, apes don't have

.....................

| Fur | Tails |
| Ears | Thumbs |

| Kitchen sponge | Toilet seat |
| Coffee mug | Sofa |

2. The ..................... usually contains more germs than any other object in your house.

| Chalk | Flint |
| Slate | Marble |

3. Ancient people made tools out of ....................., a type of very hard stone.

| 4,500 | 450 million |
| 4.5 billion | 45 billion |

4. The Earth is around ..................... years old.

5. All modern dogs are descended from .....................

| Mammoths | Wolves |
| Whales | Dinosaurs |

**6.** Located in Russia, Lake ..................
is the world's largest freshwater lake.

> Malawi   Huron
>
> Baikal   Titicaca

> Minecraft   Tetris
>
> Super Mario   Pokémon

**7.** ..................... is a video game
in which players try to capture and
collect small monsters.

**8.** Soldiers in ancient
Rome used to be partly paid in ...................

> Salt   Pepper
>
> Spices   Tea

> Five   Six
>
> Seven   Eight

**9.** There are .................. continents.

**10.** A .................. is a type
of curved stick from Australia
designed to come back when
it's thrown.

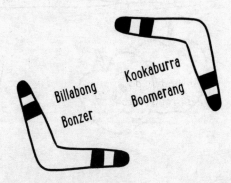

Billabong   Kookaburra

Bonzer   Boomerang

## QUIZ 6: FRUITY CONFUSION

Can you identify the fruit on this shopping list from their pictures? Write your answers in the spaces.

### SHOPPING LIST

- [ ] Watermelon
- [ ] Pear
- [ ] Grapes
- [ ] Dragon fruit
- [ ] Kiwi fruit
- [ ] Apple
- [ ] Orange
- [ ] Mangosteen
- [ ] Coconut
- [ ] Durian

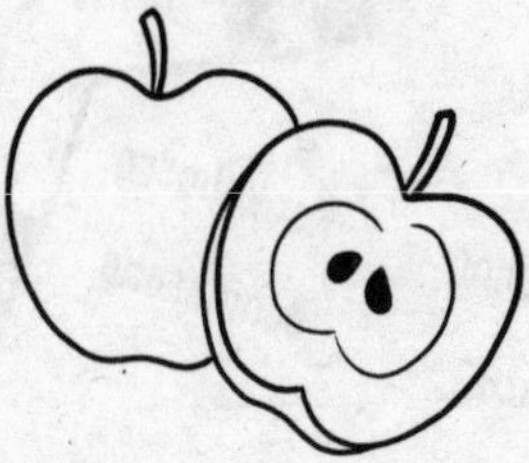

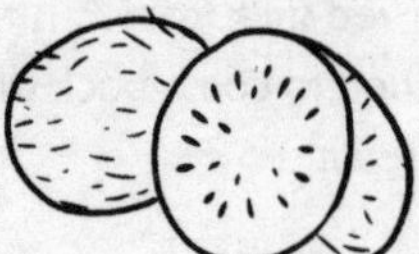

1. ..........................

2. ..........................

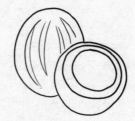

3. ...............................

4. ...............................

5. ...............................

6. ...............................

7. ...............................

8. ...............................

9. ...............................

10. ...............................

SCORE .................................

Can you pick out the right answer from the two wrong ones in this multiple choice quiz?

**1.** What sport is played at the annual Wimbledon Championships in London, UK?

**A)** Football          **B)** Tennis          **C)** Basketball

**2.** What animals are thought to be kept as pets by witches?

**A)** Black cats          **B)** Brown dogs          **C)** Yellow monkeys

**3.** How many days are there in the month of October?

**A)** 30          **B)** 31          **C)** 32

**4.** In what country was the kite invented?

**A)** USA          **B)** Italy          **C)** China

**5.** How many events make up the Olympic sport of heptathlon?

**A)** Five          **B)** Seven          **C)** Ten

**6.** A 'mermaid's purse' is the egg case of which marine animal?

**A)** Squid          **B)** Dolphin          **C)** Shark

**7.** In what city would you find the world's tallest building, the Burj Khalifa?

**A)** Dubai, UAE          **B)** New York, USA          **C)** Moscow, Russia

**8.** What part of the body has the most number of sweat glands?

**A)** Forehead          **B)** Armpits          **C)** Soles of the feet

**9.** In what month is the holiday of Thanksgiving held in the USA?

**A)** November          **B)** December          **C)** January

**10.** What is a beaver's home called?

**A)** Lodge          **B)** Inn          **C)** Hotel

Are these statements true or false? Tick your answers.

1. Barcelona is the capital of Spain.

⬭ True     False ✿

2. A baby kangaroo is called a Davey.

⬭ True     False ✿

3. The volcanic rock, pumice, is so full of air it can float on water.

⬭ True     False ✿

4. Many birds feed their chicks partly digested food.

⬭ True     False ✿

5. Nintendo is a computer game company based in Russia.

⬭ True     False ✿

6. The shortest day of the year is known as the Winter Equinox.

⬭ True     False ✿

7. The teddy bear was named after US president, Theodore Roosevelt.

⬭ True     False ✿

8. The Great Dane is the world's tallest breed of dog.

⬭ True     False ✿

9. It's impossible to see a comet in the night sky with the naked eye.

⬭ True     False ✿

10. There is no difference between crocodiles and alligators.

⬭ True     False ✿

This is a game for two or more players. One reads out the clues, while the others try to work out what is being talked about. The answer to every question is a vehicle or form of transport.

QUESTION 1.
Clue 1 (4 points): I was invented in the early 20th century.
Clue 2 (3 points): I am a type of flying vehicle.
Clue 3 (2 points): I can take off vertically (straight up).
Clue 4 (1 point): I am lifted into the air by a big spinning rotor on top of me.

QUESTION 2.
Clue 1 (4 points): I was invented in France in 1783.
Clue 2 (3 points): I am a type of slow-moving flying vehicle.
Clue 3 (2 points): I am usually round, although I can be made in lots of different shapes.
Clue 4 (1 point): People ride me stood in a hanging basket.

QUESTION 3.
Clue 1 (4 points): I can only be used by one person at a time.
Clue 2 (3 points): I have very small wheels and no motor.
Clue 3 (2 points): If not on a hill, you have to use your legs to make me go.
Clue 4 (1 point): You can use me to do tricks, such as ollies and kickflips.

QUESTION 4.
Clue 1 (4 points): I am a large, quick-moving vehicle often seen in cities.
Clue 2 (3 points): I am often painted in a bright colour such as red.
Clue 3 (2 points): I have a siren.
Clue 4 (1 point): I have ladders, and hoses for squirting water.

QUESTION 5.
Clue 1 (4 points): I am a slow-moving, four-wheeled vehicle.
Clue 2 (3 points): I have a driver but you don't see me on roads.
Clue 3 (2 points): I have two long prongs at the front that can move up and down.
Clue 4 (1 point): I am used for stacking things in factories.

## QUESTION 6.

**Clue 1 (4 points):** I am an old, traditional type of vehicle with a pointed front end and a flat back end.

**Clue 2 (3 points):** Usually made of wood, I travel on water.

**Clue 3 (2 points):** I am powered by a person.

**Clue 4 (1 point):** A pair of oars move me through the water.

## QUESTION 7.

**Clue 1 (4 points):** I was invented in the 19th century.

**Clue 2 (3 points):** I am a popular form of transport all over the world.

**Clue 3 (2 points):** I have two wheels.

**Clue 4 (1 point):** I am powered by pedals.

## QUESTION 8.

**Clue 1 (4 points):** I am a form of transport found in most major cities.

**Clue 2 (3 points):** Lots of people catch me every day.

**Clue 3 (2 points):** I used to be powered by steam.

**Clue 4 (1 point):** I travel on rails.

## QUESTION 9.

**Clue 1 (4 points):** I have four wheels.

**Clue 2 (3 points):** My back wheels are usually bigger than my front ones.

**Clue 3 (2 points):** I can pull different types of machinery, such as trailers and ploughs.

**Clue 4 (1 point):** You'll usually find me on a farm.

## QUESTION 10.

**Clue 1 (4 points):** I have four wheels.

**Clue 2 (3 points):** I can go very fast.

**Clue 3 (2 points):** I compete with other vehicles on tracks to see which one is fastest.

**Clue 4 (1 point):** My types include Formula 1 and dragsters.

Let's see who's smarter, children or adults. The questions at the top are for adults, and should be asked by kids, while the questions down below are for kids, and should be asked by adults. You can ask them all at once or take it in turns.

### QUESTIONS FOR ADULTS

**1.** What is the largest number of Oscars won by a single film?

**A)** Nine      **B)** Eleven      **C)** Thirteen

**2.** Which of these is the most recent geological period?

**A)** Permian      **B)** Cretaceous      **C)** Holocene

**3.** What is the height of a professional basketball net?

**A)** 245 cm (8 ft)      **B)** 305 cm (10 ft)      **C)** 365 cm (12 ft)

**4.** The 'twit-twoo' sound of tawny owls is actually made by two owls, one saying 'twit' and the other replying 'twoo'. True or false?

**5.** What is the name of the volcano that erupted in the USA in 1980?

**A)** Mount St. Helens      **B)** Mount St. Joans      **C)** Mount St. Vincents

### QUESTIONS FOR KIDS

**1.** The Oscars movie award ceremony is held in which city?

**A)** New York      **B)** Los Angeles      **C)** Paris

**2.** Which of these now extinct creatures was alive most recently?

**A)** *Stegosaurus*      **B)** Woolly mammoth      **C)** Dodo

**3.** A shuttlecock is used in which of these sports?

**A)** Badminton      **B)** Tennis      **C)** Lacrosse

**4.** Polar bear fur isn't actually white but see-through. True or false?

**5.** What was the name of the volcano that exploded with great force in Indonesia in 1883?

**A)** Krakatoa      **B)** Mauna Loa      **C)** Eyjafjallajökull

# Chapter 10
# WEIRD
# BUT TRUE

Tick whether you think these bizarre facts about the natural world are true or false.

1. An elephant's trunk contains around 4,000 muscles.

True    False

2. The dragon's blood tree gets its name because it has red sap.

True    False

3. There are some species of snake that can glide through the air.

True    False

4. The largest moth in the world has a wingspan of 1 metre (39 in).

True    False

5. The water in Lake Hillier in Australia is completely pink.

True    False

6. A one-day old reindeer can run faster than the fastest adult human.

True    False

7. Male proboscis monkeys have unusually small noses.

True    False

8. Vegetable sheep are plants from New Zealand that look like sheep.

True    False

9. Owls can spin their heads all the way around.

True    False

10. The eternal jellyfish can live forever.

True    False

For each of these questions, there is just one correct answer.
Circle the correct answer: A, B or C.

1. Which of these animals did the ancient Egyptians consider sacred?
A) Rabbit          B) Cat          C) Hamster

2. Which of these used to be an official Olympic sport?
A) Egg-and-spoon race   B) Tug of War   C) Three-legged race

3. Which famous author went missing in 1926 for 11 days?
A) Tove Jansson      B) J. K. Rowling   C) Agatha Christie

4. What became known as the 'devil's drink' when it first arrived in
Europe in the 16th century?
A) Coffee          B) Cola          C) Hot chocolate

5. The 14th-century king Mansu Musa, believed to be the richest
person who ever lived, was from which country?
A) Russia          B) China          C) Mali

6. How many languages did Britain's Queen Victoria speak?
A) One          B) Three          C) Five

7. Which of the following were eaten as a delicacy in ancient Rome?
A) Eagles          B) Emus          C) Flamingos

8. In 1635, Japan's ruler banned travel to or from the country. How
many years did this rule remain in place for?
A) 2 years          B) 27 years          C) 217 years

9. Which item of cutlery wasn't widely used in Britain until the 1800s?
A) Knife          B) Fork          C) Spoon

10. In medieval Europe, snail slime was used to treat what?
A) Headaches   B) Burns   C) Hayfever

In each of these lists, there's something that doesn't belong.
Can you work out what it is? Circle your answers.

1. Which of these isn't a real type of beetle?

Spider beetle          Stag beetle          Tortoise beetle

Snake beetle           Rhinoceros beetle

2. Which of these pungent plants is a fake?

Skunk cabbage          Stinking iris          Stink lily

Corpse flower          Smelly sock plant

3. Four of these are genuine types of sport, but one is make-believe –
can you pick it out?

Underwater hockey       Toe wrestling          Unicorn racing

Swamp football          Mermaiding

4. All of these items have been left by humans in space, except for one.
Can you work out what it is?

Spatula                 Frying pan             Camera

Astronaut pee           Toothbrush

5. Which of these isn't a real type of shark?

Wobbegong shark         Goblin shark           Giraffe shark

Cookiecutter shark      Carpet shark

**6.** Which four are real-life inventions and which one is made-up?

Voice-activated taps     Robot vacuum cleaner     Floating sofa

Foldable phones          Sonic toothbrush


**7.** Can you spot the fake eco-powered invention?

Plastic made from banana peel     Solar-powered cooker

Water-harvesting umbrella          Solar-powered phones

Wind-powered skateboard


**8.** Which of these dishes from around the world is the fake one?

Crispy tarantulas, Cambodia     Hundred-year-old egg, China

Poached slugs, UK               Jellied moose nose, Canada

Smoked puffin, Iceland


**9.** Can you spot the only bird that can fly among the ground dwellers?

Kakapo          Cassowary          Kiwi

Albatross       Rhea


**10.** Can you pick the fake festival from the other genuine festivals?

Bun Festival, Hong Kong           Mud Festival, South Korea

Candyfloss Festival, France       Air-Guitar Festival, Finland

Underwater Music Festival, USA

For each of these food-themed questions, there are two correct statements and one incorrect one. Can you work out which is which? Circle the one you think is a mistake.

## 1. FUN FRUITS
**A)** Dragon fruit grow on cacti.
**B)** Pineapples grow on trees.
**C)** Melons grow on vines.

## 2. SAY CHEESE!
**A)** Cheddar cheese ice cream is a popular flavour in the Philippines.
**B)** An Italian cheese called Casu Marza contains live maggots.
**C)** Cheese wasn't invented until the 20th century.

## 3. BRILLIANT BAKES
**A)** Every Christmas, a giant gingerbread city is built in Bergen, Norway.
**B)** 'Biscuit' comes from a French word meaning 'delicious smell'.
**C)** Chocolate-chip cookies were the first food to be baked in space.

## 4. PERFECT PASTA
**A)** Some types of pasta grow on trees.
**B)** The pasta penne, which means 'pen' in Italian, got its name because it looks like the tip of a fountain pen.
**C)** In the Middle Ages, pasta was often eaten sprinkled with sugar or cinnamon.

## 5. FAST FOOD
**A)** KFC is traditionally eaten on Christmas Day in Japan.
**B)** McDonald's was founded in the 17th century.
**C)** In 2016, Burger King in Israel gave customers the option to have their burger served in a doughnut instead of a bun.

## 6. REALLY OLD FOOD
**A)** A 100-year-old fruitcake was discovered in Antarctica in 2017.

**B)** A 3,200-year-old cheese was found in an Egyptian tomb in 2018.

**C)** A 300-year-old sandwich was found behind a cupboard in the UK in 2020.

## 7. VEG OF MANY COLOURS
**A)** There is a variety of carrot that is purple.

**B)** There is a variety of sweetcorn that is pink.

**C)** There is a variety of banana that is red.

## 8. HEALTH CURES?
**A)** Ketchup was originally sold as a cure for stomach problems.

**B)** Gummy bears were first created to cure toothache.

**C)** White chocolate was originally invented as a coating for vitamins.

## 9. CHOCOHOLIC
**A)** The scientific name for chocolate translates as 'food that melts in the mouth'.

**B)** The original hot chocolate drunk by the Maya people of Mexico was spicy and bitter.

**C)** The first cocoa beans to arrive in the UK in the 16$^{th}$ century were mistaken for sheep poo and burned.

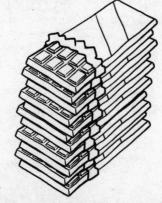

## 10. MISTAKEN IDENTITY
**A)** Avocados are actually a type of fruit.

**B)** Rhubarb is actually a type of vegetable.

**C)** Cranberries are actually a type of nut.

Can you write in the word, or words, that are missing from these statements? For each statement, the correct answer is one of the options written in the box at the side.

**A house**
**A 10-storey building**
**The Eiffel Tower**
**A mountain**

1. If a flea was human size, it could jump as high as ....................

**Shells    Pebbles**

**Fish    Diamonds**

2. Male gentoo penguins give .................... to females during courtship.

**Suitcase**
**Car**
**Single-decker bus**
**Double-decker bus**

3. ENIAC, one of the world's first computers, was roughly as big as a ....................

**1 minute    1 hour**

**1 day    1 week**

4. A cockroach can live for .................... without its head.

5. There is a famous .................... in the middle of a football pitch in Estonia.

**Statue    Tree**

**Pond    Carousel**

6. The coconut was named after an old Portuguese word for the

.....................

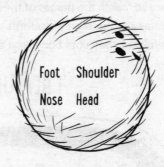

Foot   Shoulder

Nose   Head

Asia      Europe

Australia   Antarctica

7. The world's largest desert, the Sahara, covers an area bigger than the continent of

.....................

8. The first email was sent in .....................

| 1971 | 1981 |
| 1991 | 2001 |

Hairdryer   Radiator

Microwave   Toaster

9. The ..................... was accidentally invented by scientist Percy LeBaron Spencer when he was fiddling with a device and found that it had melted a chocolate bar in his pocket.

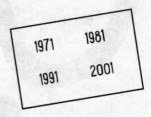

10. Instead of barking, the Basenji dog from Africa

.....................

Miaows   Yodels   Whistles   Purrs

# QUIZ 6: CURIOUS CREATURES

Can you match the names of these unusual underwater creatures to the correct pictures? Read their names carefully as they could give you a clue.

## CREATURE LIST

Anglerfish
Pufferfish
Handfish
Leafy Sea Dragon
Sea pen
Dumbo Octopus
Sea cucumber
Manta ray
Blobfish
Goblin shark

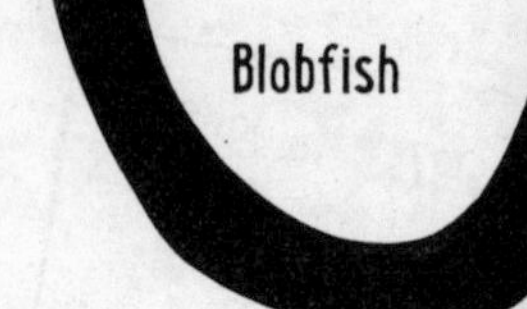

1. ..........................

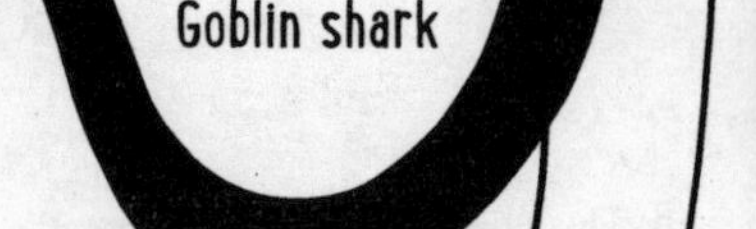

2. ..........................

3. ................................

4. ................................

5. ................................

6. ................................

7. ................................

8. ................................

9. ................................

10. ................................

Can you pick out the right answer from the two wrong ones in this multiple choice quiz?

**1.** One of the largest kite festivals in the world takes place each year on Bondi Beach in Australia. In which city would you find Bondi Beach?

**A)** Melbourne      **B)** Perth      **C)** Sydney

**2.** The world's longest tunnel slide is located in London's Queen Elizabeth Olympic Park. In what year did London last host the Olympics?

**A)** 2008      **B)** 2012      **C)** 2016

**3.** A toilet worth how much was stolen from a UK art exhibition in 2019?

**A)** £4      **B)** £40,000      **C)** £4 million

**4.** What is the name of the hip-hop musical about a US founding father?

**A)** *Hamilton*      **B)** *Washington*      **C)** *Franklin*

**5.** The oldest theme park in the world is Bakken in Copenhagen, which first opened its gates in way back in 1583. Which country is Copenhagen in?

**A)** Sweden      **B)** Denmark      **C)** Germany

**6.** In ancient Rome, the emperors' togas were coloured with a rich purple dye obtained from which type of animal?

**A)** Sea snails      **B)** Land snails      **C)** Spiders

**7.** *Toy Story 2* was almost deleted when a member of staff wiped Pixar's computer system. What is the name of the cowgirl in *Toy Story 2*?

**A)** Julie      **B)** Jessie      **C)** Jaimie

**8.** *Where the Wild Things Are* was originally going to be about which animals (until the author realised he couldn't draw them very well)?

**A)** Giraffes      **B)** Dogs      **C)** Horses

**9.** What type of celestial object has been named after Bilbo Baggins?

**A)** Asteroid      **B)** Comet      **C)** Planet

**10.** At their closest point, how far apart are the USA and Russia?

**A)** 3.8 km (2.4 miles)      **B)** 380 km (236 miles)      **C)** 3,800 km (2,361 miles)

Are these statements true or false? Tick your answers.

1. The Moon is the coldest place in the Solar System.

True    False

2. Scientists have worked out exactly how many stars there are in space.

True    False

3. The largest canyon in the Solar System is located on Saturn.

True    False

4. It takes Neptune ten Earth years to orbit the Sun.

True    False

5. The dwarf planet Pluto was named by an 11-year-old girl.

True    False

6. Venus's day is longer than its year.

True    False

7. Some comets have tails that are 160 million km (99 million miles) long.

True    False

8. Astronauts left a park bench on the Moon.

True    False

9. It is thought to rain diamonds on Jupiter.

True    False

10. Footprints on the Moon will be there for millions of years.

True    False

This is a game for two or more players. One reads out the clues, while the others try to work out who or what is being talked about. Add up the points at the end – the player with the most is the winner.

QUESTION 1.
Clue 1 (4 points): I have cube-shaped poo.
Clue 2 (3 points): I am a marsupial (my babies develop in a pouch).
Clue 3 (2 points): I live in Australia.
Clue 4 (1 point): I look a bit like a small, stocky bear.

QUESTION 2.
Clue 1 (4 points): I am a building with 132 rooms and 35 bathrooms.
Clue 2 (3 points): These include a room called the Oval Office.
Clue 3 (2 points): I am located in Washington, D.C.
Clue 4 (1 point): I am the home of the president of the USA.

QUESTION 3.
Clue 1 (4 points): I became a king when I was just 9 years old.
Clue 2 (3 points): I was buried in three coffins, one made of gold.
Clue 3 (2 points): My tomb is located in the Valley of the Kings.
Clue 4 (1 point): I am one of the most famous Egyptian pharaohs.

QUESTION 4.
Clue 1 (4 points): I live in rainforests in Africa.
Clue 2 (3 points): I use smelly glands on my hooves to mark my territory.
Clue 3 (2 points): I have a long, purple-black tongue and a striped behind.
Clue 4 (1 point): I look like a cross between a zebra and a giraffe.

QUESTION 5.
Clue 1 (4 points): It took my ladies in waiting four hours a day to dress and undress me.
Clue 2 (3 points): I have been portrayed on film and in TV shows more often than any other British monarch.
Clue 3 (2 points): I was only the second woman to be Queen of England.
Clue 4 (1 point): My dad was Henry VIII and my mum was Anne Boleyn.

## QUESTION 6.
**Clue 1 (4 points):** I am the second brightest object in Earth's night sky.
**Clue 2 (3 points):** I am the most expensive structure ever built.
**Clue 3 (2 points):** I contain two bathrooms, a gym and over 50 computers.
**Clue 4 (1 point):** Astronauts have been living on me since 1998.

## QUESTION 7.
**Clue 1 (4 points):** I am a song originally composed in 1893.
**Clue 2 (3 points):** The *Curiosity* rover on Mars hummed my tune to itself on a special day in 2013.
**Clue 3 (2 points):** I am one of the most frequently sung songs in the English language.
**Clue 4 (1 point):** You sing me when blowing out the candles on your cake.

## QUESTION 8.
**Clue 1 (4 points):** I don't have any eyebrows.
**Clue 2 (3 points):** I regularly receive fan mail and poems from admirers even though I'm over 500 years old.
**Clue 3 (2 points):** I have my own room in the Louvre Museum in Paris.
**Clue 4 (1 point):** I was painted by Leonardo da Vinci.

## QUESTION 9.
**Clue 1 (4 points):** I am the first country in the world to have created a landing pad for UFOs.
**Clue 2 (3 points):** I stretch across six time zones.
**Clue 3 (2 points):** I am home to 62% of all the world's lakes.
**Clue 4 (1 point):** I share a border with just one country – the USA.

## QUESTION 10.
**Clue 1 (4 points):** I am a bird with over 300 species.
**Clue 2 (3 points):** My young are called 'squabs'.
**Clue 3 (2 points):** I was used to carry messages in both world wars.
**Clue 4 (1 point):** My most common species is found cities across the world.

Let's see who's smarter, children or adults. The questions at the top are for adults, and should be asked by kids, while the questions down below are for kids, and should be asked by adults. You can ask them all at once or take it in turns.

## QUESTIONS FOR ADULTS

1. Which of these animals can shrink its brain in winter to help it conserve energy?
A) Shrew    B) Ferret    C) Badger

2. The size of a grain of rice, what is the human body's smallest gland?
A) Thyroid gland    B) Pancreas    C) Pineal gland

3. The Great Fire of London began in Pudding Lane. Where did it end?
A) Bread Street    B) Pye Corner    C) Dessert Avenue

4. If Mount Everest was placed inside the Marianas Trench, the deepest part of the ocean, its summit wouldn't reach the surface. True or false?

5. Pato, Argentina's national game, is named after which bird?
A) Duck    B) Chicken    C) Penguin

## QUESTIONS FOR KIDS

1. Brown bears can eat up to 40,000 of what creature in a single day?
A) Salmon    B) Moths    C) Reindeer

2. Sometimes over 1 m (39 in) long, what are the longest cells in the body?
A) Red blood cells    B) Liver cells    C) Nerve cells (neurons)

3. Shakespeare died the same day he was born, 23 April, in what year?
A) 1216    B) 1616    C) 1916

4. The pieces of rock that make up the Earth's crust are moving as fast as your fingernails grow. True or false?

5. Despite their name, Olympic gold medals are made of which metal?
A) Silver    B) Bronze    C) Tin

ANSWERS

# CHAPTER 1: ANIMALS AND NATURE

## Quiz 1: True or False

1. True    2. False (it's the whale shark)    3. False (they live near the North Pole)    4. True (that's the longest of any animal)    5. True    6. False (camels store fat in their hump)    7. True (that's the same as you lifting up a car)    8. False (it's known as a 'tower')    9. True    10. True (the cheetah is the fastest land animal, but the fastest animal overall is the peregrine falcon which can dive at 390 kph (242 mph))

## Quiz 2: Multiple Choice

1. B) Redwoods    2. B) Feet (which, strangely enough, is where most of their tastebuds are located)    3. C) Blue whale (it can measure up to 30 m long and weigh over 170 tonnes)    4. A) Ostrich (which can run up to 70 kph (43 mph))    5. B) Insects    6. C) Dragon    7. B) Sap    8. A) Spiders    9. C) Oceania    10. A) Pea crab

## Quiz 3: Odd One Out

1. Manatee    2. Jaguar    3. Hairy eagle    4. Prickly pear tree (it's a type of cactus)    5. Purple bear    6. Walrus    7. Giant centipede    8. Samba (which is a type of dance; a mamba is a type of snake)    9. France    10. Camel

## Quiz 4: Spot the Mistake

1. C (sharks breathe through their gills)    2. B (koalas are marsupials)    3. A    4. C (they do have purple tongues, but they have just two horns on their heads)    5. B    6. A    7. B (there are around 250 species of marsupial)    8. C (bulls are partially colour blind and can't see the colour red)    9. B (tigers don't have permanent homes)    10. C (chameleons can change colour, but they do it to signal to each other, not for camouflage)

## Quiz 5: Creature Connections

1. Big cats    2. Monkeys    3. Seabirds    4. Lizards    5. Bats    6. Sharks    7. Birds of prey    8. Penguins    9. Sea turtles    10. Seals

## Quiz 6: Animal Match-Ups

1. South America   2. Antarctica   3. Asia   4. North America
5. Oceania   6. Asia   7. North America   8. Africa
9. Oceania   10. South America

## Quiz 7: Natural Knowledge

1. A) Whale (the bowhead whale to be precise)   2. C) Giant squid
3. B) 5 km (3 miles)   4. A) Bamboo   5. B) Foal   6. C) Saltwater
crocodile   7. A) Chihuahua   8. B) Hummingbird   9. B) 8
10. B) Monkey puzzle tree

## Quiz 8: All About Cats

1. A) Cubs   2. C) 24 (12 on each side)   3. B) Ocelot
4. B) Cheetah   5. A) Egypt   6. C) Italy   7. A) Oranges (and,
indeed, any citrus fruit)   8. C) 15 hours (they like their rest)
9. B) Leopard   10. C) 38

## Quiz 9: Who or What Am I?

1. Honey bee   2. Owl   3. Wolf   4. Crab   5. Hippopotamus   6.
Penguin   7. Dolphin   8. Flamingo   9. Goliath birdeater spider (or
tarantula)   10. Hyena

## Quiz 10: Adults vs Kids

**Adults**: 1. C) Sperm whale   2. B) Parliament   3. B) Polar bear
4. False (it's made of keratin, the same substance that makes up hair
and nails)   5. C) Three (the third one is located in the inner corner
of the eye and sweeps across the eyes below the other two to add an
extra layer of protection)

**Kids**: 1. A) Ostrich   2. C) Pride   3. C) African elephant   4. False
(many mammals, such as whales and dolphins, live in the sea)   5. B) 8

# CHAPTER 2: SCIENCE AND TECHNOLOGY

## Quiz 1: True or False

1. True   2. False (H is the symbol for hydrogen)   3. False (the study of birds is known as ornithology)   4. True   5. False (it's nitrogen, which makes up about 78% of the atmosphere; oxygen makes up 21%)   6. True (a lightning bolt can reach 30,000°C or five times hotter than the surface of the Sun at 6,000°C)   7. True   8. False (it's caused by a virus)   9. True   10. True (gold is much denser than silver, so an object made of gold is heavier than one of the same size made of silver)

## Quiz 2: Multiple Choice

1. B) Chlorophyll   2. B) China   3. C) $H_2O$   4. A) Alternating Current   5. B) Rocks   6. B) World Wide Web   7. C) The Sun   8. A) Diamonds   9. B) Conductor   10. C) Insulator

## Quiz 3: Odd One Out

1. Helium   2. Farmology   3. Stratoaltrobus   4. Pinestone   5. Isaac Futon   6. Chrysler   7. Maelstrom   8. Bubonic   9. Megasphere   10. Nanometre

## Quiz 4: Spot the Mistake

1. B (the speed of light is very fast, around 300,000 km (190,000 miles) per second)   2. C (someone who studies chemistry is a chemist)   3. C (penguins may live where it's very cold but they have warm blood)   4. B (an animal that eats plants is a herbivore)   5. A (lightning can, and sometimes does, strike the same place twice)   6. C (a material that cannot be seen through is opaque)   7. A (the prairie dog is actually a type of rodent)   8. B   9. A (the aeroplane was invented in the USA)   10. C (cows take in oxygen, just like human beings do, but they do also release methane)

## Quiz 5: Fill in the Blanks

1. Trees   2. Maglev (it stands for 'magnetic levitation')   3. Tsunami   4. Crust   5. Evaporates   6. Emerald   7. Hydrogen   8. 500 years   9. Contract   10. Venus fly trap

## Quiz 6: Science Match-Ups

1. Aeroplane: The Wright Brothers    2. Television: John Logie Baird    3. Cereal Flakes: John Harvey Kellogg
4. Motor Car: Karl Benz    5. Light bulb: Thomas Edison
6. *Ichthyosaurus*: Mary Anning    7. Printing press: Johannes Gutenberg    8. Dynamite: Alfred Nobel    9. Radium and Polonium: Marie Curie    10. World Wide Web: Tim Berners-Lee

## Quiz 7: Science Savvy

1. C) Gravity    2. B) Earthquakes    3. C) $E = MC^2$
4. A) Photosynthesis    5. C) Salt    6. B) Filament    7. B) Igneous    8. C) Motorbike    9. B) North and South    10. B) Stalagmites

## Quiz 8: Number Knowledge

1. A) 8 minutes    2. A) 19th    3. C) 1,000    4. C) 95%
5. C) 4,400 million years old (or 4.4 billion years old)    6. A) 1 (the very first one set up by the people who invented the web)    7. B) 7
8. B) 3.14    9. B) 1973    10. B) 1,227 kph (762.4 mph)

## Quiz 9: Who or What Am I?

1. Glass    2. Computer    3. Air    4. Metal    5. Albert Einstein
6. Atom    7. Seed    8. Battery    9. Cell    10. Earth

## Quiz 10: Adults vs Kids

**Adults**: 1. B) Helicopter    2. A) Noble gases    3. B) Intense
4. True (he was an Italian-American inventor who developed the whirlpool bath in the 1960s)    5. B) Meteorologist

**Kids**: 1. B) Hot-air balloon    2. A) Periodic Table    3. C) Silicon
4. False (it was invented by Charles Babbage, a British engineer who built the first mechanical computer in the early 19th century)
5. B) Botanist

# CHAPTER 3: SPACE

## Quiz 1: True or False

1. False (there are eight planets in the Solar System)    2. True
3. False (Jupiter is the biggest planet in the Solar System. Mercury is the smallest)    4. True    5. False (Venus is the hottest planet in the Solar System. Uranus is the coldest)    6. False (Jupiter, Uranus and Neptune also have rings, they're just much fainter)    7. True (and it's been there for at least 300 years)    8. True (it's called Olympus Mons and it's about two and a half times taller than Earth's biggest mountain, Everest)    9. False (the Sun is mainly made up of gas)    10. False (comets, which are lumps of ice and dust with a long streaming tail of gas, come from the outer reaches of the Solar System, way beyond Uranus, and make long orbits around the Sun)

## Quiz 2: Moon Multiple Choice

1. B) 1969    2. A) Craters    3. C) Neil Armstrong
4. B) Apollo    5. C) Seas    6. C) Golf (he took up a club and hit a couple of balls to see how far they'd fly in the weaker gravity on the Moon's surface)    7. C) Twelve (six missions of two astronauts each)
8. A) Eagle    9. B) Mankind 10. C) 385,000 km (239,228 miles)

## Quiz 3: Odd One Out

1. Europa    2. Tigris    3. Green Giant    4. Keyboard    5. Peel
6. Death Star (that's from *Star Wars*)    7. USS *Enterprise* (that's from *Star Trek*)    8. Saturn    9. U-turn    10. Pluto

## Quiz 4: Spot the Mistake

1. C (the Sun goes out of sight; it doesn't turn black)    2. B (Venus doesn't have any moons)    3. A (the Moon has almost no atmosphere)
4. C (Jupiter has been visited by nine spacecraft)    5. C (Over 30 monkeys have travelled into space)    6. A (there are countless billions of stars in the Universe)    7. B (the gases in Neptune's atmosphere give it a bluish colour)    8. C (Mercury doesn't produce its own light; it reflects light from the Sun)    9. A (sound is formed by waves in air, and as there's no air in the vacuum of space, there can be no sound; light can travel through a vacuum; and smells are made of particles that can travel into a vacuum)    10. B (Mars has almost no liquid water)

## Quiz 5: Fill in the Blanks

1. Red   2. Gravity   3. *Saturn 5*   4. Milky Way   5. Venus
6. Big Bang   7. Laika   8. Earth   9. Russia   10. Halley's

## Quiz 6: Space Match-Ups

1. The Sun   2. Mercury   3. Venus   4. The Moon   5. Earth
6. Mars   7. Jupiter   8. Saturn   9. Uranus   10. Neptune

## Quiz 7: Astro Awareness

1. B) Yuri Gagarin   2. B) 1961   3. C) Black hole   4. A) NASA
5. C) Ice and dust   6. A) Hubble (it was named after a famous
American astronomer, Edwin Hubble)   7. C) 8 months
8. A) Meteor   9. C) Dwarf planet   10. B) Space walk

## Quiz 8: Space Stuff

1. True (the Moon rotates once every time it orbits the Earth, so we
always see the same side)   2. False (it's much bigger)   3. True
4. False (Mars has two moons)   5. True   6. True (in 1963)
7. False (it was Apollo 11)   8. True (the lack of gravity helps them to
stretch out)   9. False (it has a thin atmosphere, mainly made of carbon
dioxide)   10. C) True (the gas and dust in a comet are released in
slightly different ways, forming two tails)

## Quiz 9: Who or What Am I?

1. Saturn   2. Neil Armstrong   3. The Sun   4. Pluto
5. Telescope   6. Constellation   7. The Moon
8. The Milky Way   9. Crater   10. Rocket

## Quiz 10: Adults vs Kids

**Adults:** 1. C) Mars and Jupiter   2. B) Jupiter   3. B) 1981
4. False (it stands for 'Aeronautics'. It's the National Aeronautics and
Space Administration)   5. A) Transit

**Kids:** 1. A) Venus   2. B) Jupiter
3. B) 1957   4. True   5. C) Eclipse

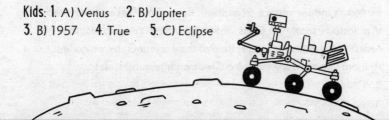

# CHAPTER 4: HISTORY

## Quiz 1: True or False

1. False (Henry VIII had six wives)    2. True (he won them in the 100 m, 200 m, 4 x 100 m relay, and long jump)    3. False (a samurai was a warrior in medieval Japan)    4. True    5. False (a gladiator was a warrior who fought battles in front of crowds as a form of entertainment)    6. True.    7. False (it was invented in the 19th century)    8. True.    9. False (it began in 1914)    10. True (they came from Denmark, Norway and Sweden)

## Quiz 2: Multiple Choice

1. B) Jolly Roger    2. C) Elephants    3. A) Zeus    4. B) Air Force One    5. C) Hun    6. A) Penny Black    7. A) Round    8. B) The Dreamtime    9. C) Bronze Age    10. B) Cleopatra

## Quiz 3: Odd One Out

1. Odin    2. Winston Churchill    3. Outer Ages    4. Julius Caesar
5. Saxons    6. Newton    7. James III (there was a King Stephen)
8. Horned beaver    9. King    10. Zero

## Quiz 4: Spot the Mistake

1. B (despite many people believing it to be true, the Great Wall cannot be seen from space – astronauts have tried looking)
2. C (its furthest extent was actually marked by a place called Pye Corner)    3. B (the French Revolution took place in the 18th century)
4. A (most medieval castles were built at the top of a hill so they could be easily defended)    5. B (King Arthur was helped by a wizard called Merlin)    6. C (Captain Cook was not the first person to set foot on Australian soil. Aboriginal Australians have been living there for over 50,000 years)    7. B (World War I started in Europe)
8. B (Mahatma Gandhi was a politician and activist who campaigned for India's independence from British Rule)    9. A (The Thirty Years War lasted exactly 30 years, but the Hundred Years War lasted 116 years)    10. A (the writing system of the ancient Greeks is called Ancient Greek; Corinthian is a Greek architectural style)

## Quiz 5: Fill in the Blanks

1. Terrible   2. Fertile   3. Wolf   4. Wall   5. 5,000   6. Cold
7. Silk   8. Barack Obama   9. Portcullis   10. Pompeii

## Quiz 6: Timeline Trivia

1. Great Pyramid of Giza   2. Colosseum   3. Angkor Wat
4. Machu Picchu   5. Taj Mahal   6. Big Ben   7. Eiffel Tower
8. Empire State Building   9. Sydney Opera House   10. Burj Khalifa

## Quiz 7: Ancient Awareness

1. A) Kings   2. B) Black   3. C) Japan   4. B) Cuba   5. C) 1953
6. A) Alexander the Great   7. B) Zulu Kingdom   8. C) Iraq
9. B) New Zealand   10. C) Red

## Quiz 8: History or Mystery?

1. True   2. False (it's Easter Island, or Rapa Nui, that's home to the
giant stone heads)   3. True   4. False (it was caused by the bites of
infected rat fleas)   5. True   6. True   7. False (he went to China
and other Asian countries in the Middle Ages)   8. True (the Suez
Canal opened in 1869 while the Panama Canal opened in 1914)
9. False (it ended in 1945)   10. C) True

## Quiz 9: Who or What am I?

1. Abraham Lincoln   2. The Leaning Tower of Pisa   3. Charles
Darwin   4. The Statue of Liberty   5. Cleopatra   6. Nelson
Mandela   7. The Great Wall of China   8. Elizabeth I
9. The Sphinx   10. Martin Luther King Jr

## Quiz 10: Adults vs Kids

**Adults:** 1. C) Longships   2. B) Ukraine   3. A) Spring
4. True   5. B) Asia (and he never changed his mind)

**Kids:** 1. C) Gondolas   2. B) UK   3. A) Gunpowder
4. True   5. B) 1492

# CHAPTER 5: DINOSAURS

## Quiz 1: True or False

1. False (*Stegosaurus* was a gentle plant-eater)    2. True (*Triceratops* name means 'three horn face')    3. False (dinosaurs died out long before humans arrived on the scene)    4. True.    5. False (a mammoth is a type of extinct mammal)    6. True (back in 1824)    7. False.    8. True (*Plesiosaurus* lived at the same time as dinosaurs but was a different kind of reptile)    9. True (birds are the only type of dinosaur to have survived to the modern day)    10. False (*Microraptor* was a tiny feathered dinosaur)

## Quiz 2: Multiple Choice

1. A) Reptiles    2. B) Thumb (although when it was discovered, scientists originally put the spike on its nose)    3. A) *Jurassic Park*    4. A) Triassic    5. C) King    6. B) Sauropods    7. A) Pegs    8. A) *Stegosaurus* (which lived 150 million years ago; *Iguanodon* lived 125 million years ago and *Tyrannosaurus* lived 66 million years ago. Strange as it may seem, we're closer in time to *Tyrannosaurus* than it was to *Stegosaurus*)    9. C) North America    10. B) Fly

## Quiz 3: Odd One Out

1. *Parasaurolophus*    2. *Troodon*    3. *Giganotosaurus*    4. *Diplodocus*    5. *Triceratops*    6. *Tarbosaurus*    7. *Spinosaurus*    8. *Frozen*    9. *Albertosaurus*    10. *Hadrosaurus*

## Quiz 4: Spot the Mistake

1. C (fossils of food preserved inside dinosaurs are known as consumulites)    2. B (kangaroos didn't emerge until around 20 million years ago, well after the dinosaurs died out)    3. A (*Stegosaurus* had a very small brain about the size of a lime)    4. A (*Ankylosaurus* lived in the Cretaceous Period, around 68 million years ago)    5. C (dinosaurs have not been brought back to life, except in the movies)    6. B (its name actually means 'arm lizard' because it had very long front legs)    7. B (*Ichthyosaurus* hunted at sea)    8. C (it's believed that *Quetzalcoatlus* could actually fly)    9. B (modern whales are the largest sea creatures of all time)    10. C (Baby *Tyrannosaurus* didn't have wings, but it probably had feathers)

## Quiz 5: Fill in the Blanks
1. 66  2. Paleontology  3. Terrible lizard
4. *Godzilla*  5. 245  6. Dragon bones  7. North
America  8. Park  9. *Utahraptor*  10. Small

## Quiz 6: Silhouette Solutions
1. *Pteranodon*  2. *Tyrannosaurus*  3. *Iguanodon*
4. *Stegosaurus*  5. *Parasaurolophus*  6. *Brachiosaurus*
7. *Spinosaurus*  8. *Ankylosaurus*  9. *Velociraptor*  10. *Mosasaurus*

## Quiz 7: Tyrannosaurus Test
1. C) Cretaceous  2. A) North America  3. B) Tyrant lizard
4. B) 7,000 kg (15,400 lbs)  5. A) 20 kph (12 mph)  6. B) 20 cm (8 in)
7. C) *Spinosaurus*  8. B) 1902  9. B) Sue  10. C) $32 million

## Quiz 8: Dino Deduction
1. True (the first flying insects appeared around 400 million years ago)
2. False (most dinosaurs were herbivores)  3. False (dinosaurs laid
eggs)  4. False (scientists have managed to work out the colours of
some dinosaurs, but not all)  5. True  6. True  7. True  8. True
9. False (Sauropods had relatively small skulls. Ceratopsians, such as
*Triceratops*, had the largest skulls.)  10. C) False (it was invented by
the scientist Richard Owen)

## Quiz 9: Who or What am I?
1. *Tyrannosaurus*  2. *Stegosaurus*  3. *Triceratops* horn  4. Dinosaur
Museum  5. Triassic Period  6. *Iguanodon*  7. *Argentinosaurus*
8. Paleontologist  9. *Archaeopteryx*  10. Fossil

## Quiz 10: Adults vs Kids
**Adults:** 1. B) *Irritator*  2. A) England  3. B) Mesozoic  4. True
5. A) On its tail (he was very embarrassed when other scientists
pointed out his mistake)

**Kids:** 1. B) *Bambiraptor*  2. A) Pangaea  3. C) An asteroid striking
Earth  4. False (Scientists used to believe that some dinosaurs, such as
*Stegosaurus*, had a second brain near their hips, which controlled the
back half of the body. This has now been shown to be false.)
5. B) *Thagomizer* (the name was invented by a cartoonist for a joke
and then stuck)

# CHAPTER 6: TRAVEL AND GEOGRAPHY

## Quiz 1: True or False

1. False (it's Washington D.C.)   2. True   3. True   4. False (it's Portuguese)   5. True   5. False (it's Russia)   7. True   8. True
9. False (it's the Sahara)   10. True

## Quiz 2: Multiple Choice

1. C) 71%   2. B) Euro (it used to be the franc)   3. A) Disneyland
4. B) Rainforest   5. C) Canberra   6. A) Italy   7. B) Angkor Wat
8. C) Pacific   9. A) Angel Falls   10. B) USA (in New York City)

## Quiz 3: What's Missing?

Group 1. Antarctica   Group 2. Southern   Group 3. Mississippi
Group 4. Kalahari   Group 5. K2   Group 6. Sweden   Group 7. Cuba
Group 8. Chile   Group 9. Thailand   Group 10. Liberia

## Quiz 4: Spot the Mistake

1. C (the capital of Brazil is Brasilia)   2. A (there's no such language as Indian; the official languages of India are Hindi, English and 21 other languages)   3. B (the currency of Italy is the euro; the lira was its former currency)   4. B (Indonesia is the southernmost country in Asia)   5. C (the 2016 Olympic Games were held in Rio de Janeiro)
6. B (Lake Victoria is the world's largest tropical lake; it doesn't freeze)
7. B (Wurst is from Europe, but it's sausage not pickled cabbage; that's sauerkraut)   8. C (Bangkok is the capital city of Thailand)
9. B (the Andes are a mountain range in South America)
10. A (there's no such festival as the Olivetina where people throw olives, although there is a Tomatina festival in Spain where people throw tomatoes at each other)

## Quiz 5: Fill in the Blanks

1. Pound   2. Superior   3. Four   4. Asia   5. Siberian   6. Geyser
7. Star   8. Heart   9. Vatican City   10. Ten

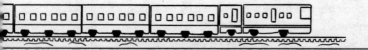

## Quiz 6: Linking the Landmarks
1. UK   2. Brazil   3. Egypt   4. Australia   5. Tanzania   6. China
7. USA   8. Greece   9. Spain   10. Russia

## Quiz 7: Geographic Guesses
1. C) Africa   2. A) Australia   3. B) Star Wars   4. C) Reykjavik
5. A) Bullet trains   6. B) The White House   7. C) England and France
8. A) The South Pole   9. A) Jumbo Jet   10. B) Day of the Dead

## Quiz 8: Travel Trivia
1. True (it's named after the Golden Gate Strait over which it stands)
2. False (it used to be and it's still Turkey's largest city, but the capital is now Ankara)   3. True (much of Mexico City was built on a lake and many houses are slowly sinking into the mud)   4. False (the USA doesn't have an official language)   5. True   6. False (it's Ottawa)
7. True (it's in the Pacific Ocean, and measures 10,984 m at its deepest point)   8. True (although the mountain itself is smaller, Mount Chimborazo lies closer to the Equator than Everest, where the Earth is at its thickest, meaning it sticks out further from the centre of the Earth)
9. False (it's known as the 'Festival of Lights')   10. C) True (it holds as much water as the next six largest rivers combined)

## Quiz 9: What Country Am I?
1. USA   2. Japan   3. Argentina   4. China   5. Russia
6. United Kingdom   7. France   8. South Africa   9. New Zealand
10. Greece

## Quiz 10: Adults vs Kids
**Adults:** 1. A) Mount Fuji   2. B) Jakarta   3. B) Africa   4. True
5. B) Tropic of Cancer

**Kids:** 1. A) The Outback   2. B) Rome   3. B) Asia   4. True
5. Equator

# CHAPTER 7: THE ARTS

## Quiz 1: True or False

1. True    2. False (there are seven novels in the Harry Potter series)
3. False (the Louvre is in Paris, France)    4. False (Sir Christopher
Wren was a famous British architect)    5. False (the space ranger is
called Buzz Lightyear)    6. True (they are known as primary colours)
7. False (he is famous for his abstract paintings)    8. True
9. False (he is famous for his paintings of water lillies)
10. False (there are two other parts, making three parts in total)

## Quiz 2: Multiple Choice

1. A) Edinburgh    2. B) Stone    3. C) Mexico    4. B) Tap
5. C) Shell    6. A) Fables    7. A) Frame    8. C) Narnia
9. B) Collage    10. B) Quills

## Quiz 3: Odd One Out

1. Madonna    2. Paddington    3. Feathers    4. Spanner
5. Steven Spielberg    6. Billy Bomblefool    7. Impersonationism
8. Max (who was the main character in *Where the Wild Things Are* by
Maurice Sendak)    9. Haute Couture (it's a term for high-class fashion
items)    10. *Peter Pan*

## Quiz 4: Spot the Mistake

1. C (*The Gruffalo* was written by Julia Donaldson)    2. B (he belongs
to Gryffindor house)    3. C (to get green, you need to mix blue
and yellow)    4. A (Michelangelo was born in Italy)    5. B (the
Rijksmuseum is in Amsterdam, Netherlands)    6. B (you press the
shutter button to take a photo)    7. A (*Tangled*'s main character is
called Rapunzel)    8. B (the word 'Renaissance' means 'Rebirth')    9.
A (the secret identity of the superhero Batman is Bruce Wayne; Bruce
Banner is the Hulk)    10. C (Carnegie Hall is a concert venue in New
York, USA)

## Quiz 5: Fill in the Blanks

1. Architects    2. Prado    3. Apple    4. Graffiti    5. Scarecrow
6. Pearl    7. Action!    8. Cut!    9. Clocks    10. 101

## Quiz 6: Art Check

1. Mechanical pencil   2. Eraser   3. Palette   4. Airbrush
5. Oil paints   6. Easel   7. Palette knife   8. Paintbrush   9. Canvas
10. Watercolour paints

## Quiz 7: Painterly Posers

1. B) Dancer   2. A) Animals   3. B) Caterpillar   4. C) Smile
5. B) Wax   6. A) Smaug   7. C) Cubism   8. C) Ballet dancers
9. A) Springfield   10. B) Hercule Poirot

## Quiz 8: Cultural Clues

1. True (Leonardo, Michelangelo, Donatello and Raphael)   2. False
(it's called *The Phantom of the Opera*).   3. False (he had a tiger
friend called Tigger)   4. True   5. False (it's a type of paint made
with eggs)   6. True   7. True (it was first used by a critic to describe
the work of the French painter, Monet)   8. False (although he did
spend much of his life in Spain)   9. False (he's from Peru)
10. C) True

## Quiz 9: Which Artist am I?

1. Leonardo da Vinci   2. Beyoncé   3. William Shakespeare
4. Vincent Van Gogh   5. Hans Christian Anderson
6. Kanye West   7. Ludwig van Beethoven   8. Beatrix Potter
9. J. K. Rowling   10. Taylor Swift

## Quiz 10: Adults vs Kids

**Adults:** 1. B) Palme d'Or   2. A) *Wave*   3. B) 14
4. False (he's from the UK)   5. C) David Hockney

**Kids:** 1. B) Oscars   2. A) *Scream*   3. B) Five
4. False (he was from Spain)   5. C) *Canterbury*

# CHAPTER 8: THE HUMAN BODY

## Quiz 1: True or False

1. True    2. False (it's red, both inside and outside your body)
3. True (the skin of an average adult weighs around 4.5 kg, while the next largest organ, the liver, weighs just 1.5 kg)    4. True (it's a nerve called the ulnar nerve which crosses your elbow)    5. False (Adults have fewer bones in their bodies. Adults have 206 bones, while babies have around 300, which gradually fuse together as they get older.)
6. False (your brain controls all the other organs in your body)
7. True (the lens bends light creating an upside down image on the retina at the back of the eye. The brain then flips the image the right way up)    8. True (it's very rare, but babies are occasionally born with one or more teeth, called natal teeth)    9. False (brown is the most common human eye colour)    10. True (there are 27 bones in each hand and 26 in each foot, making a total of 106 out of 206)

## Quiz 2: Multiple Choice

1. A) Heart    2. C) Nose    3. B) Enamel    4. A) Marrow
5. C) Saliva    6. B) Tendons    7. B) Masseter (it can close the jaws with a force of 25 kg)    8. B) 5 litres    9. A) Ears    10. A) 0–2 years

## Quiz 3: Odd One Out

1. Pancreas    2. Pulmonary    3. Vertebra    4. Electric    5. Tibia
6. Stick    7. Kidneys    8. Spleen    9. Triceps    10. Lid

## Quiz 4: Spot the Mistake

1. B (it's the opposite way round; lungs take in oxygen and expel carbon dioxide)    2. C (mucus is generally clear but may become green if you have an infection, such as a cold)    3. A (teeth don't keep growing; we only get two sets during a lifetime)    4. C (the hardest substance in the body is tooth enamel)    5. C (there are over 120 muscles in the spine; they help it to flex)    6. A (your hair grows around 10–15 cm a year)
7. C (eyelashes stop particles from getting in your eyes)
8. A (men and women have the same number of ribs: 24, or 12 pairs)
9. C (most people have just one liver)    10. C (tastebuds are not arranged in groups; all tastebuds can sense all tastes)

## Quiz 5: Fill in the Blanks

1. Nerves    2. Arteries    3. 50–100    4. Femur (thigh bone)
5. 160 kph (99 mph)    6. 100,000    7. Melanin    8. Tennis court
9. 3.5 mm (or 0.1 mm a day)    10. Oesophagus

## Quiz 6: Body Builder

1. Lungs    2. Femur    3. Brain    4. Eye    5. Heart    6. Kidneys
7. Large intestine    8. Liver    9. Pancreas    10. Stomach

## Quiz 7: Body Brainteasers

1. A) Back of the thighs    2. B) Circulatory system    3. C) Ball and
socket joint    4. C) Ear    5. B) Ligaments    6. B) Reflex
7. C) 20%    8. A) Pupil    9. C) DNA    10. A) In bones (in the bone
marrow, in fact)

## Quiz 8: Anatomical Answers

1. True    2. True (the small intestine is around 6 m long; the large
intestine around 1.5 m)    3. False (an adult brain weighs around
1.4 kg)    4. False (you have fewer teeth as a child, 24, than as an
adult, 32)    5. False (there's a tissue at the bottom of your mouth
called the *frenulum linguae* which holds the tongue in place)
6. False (there are five basic senses: touch, sight, hearing, smell and
taste)    7. True    8. True (the other type of cells, called rods,
detect light and dark but not colour)    9. True    10. False

## Quiz 9: What am I?

1. Skeleton    2. Lungs    3. Nostrils    4. Tongue    5. Liver    6. Brain
7. Thumb    8. Heart    9. Kneecap    10. Ears

## Quiz 10: Adults vs Kids

**Adults: 1.** A) Small intestine    2. A) Bile    3. B) Paediatrician
4. True    5. C) Cardiac

**Kids: 1.** A) Mouth (with chewing and saliva, which
starts the process of breaking down food)
2. A) Retina    3. B) Skin    4. True
5. C) Capillaries

# CHAPTER 9: POT LUCK

## Quiz 1: True or False

1. False (it's the opposite, in fact; all snowflakes are unique)
2. True (it's called 'echolocation')   3. False (there are a thousand)
4. False (it travels much slower – sound travels at 343 metres per second, while light travels at 299 million metres per second)
5. True   6. False (they're called pups)   7. True (by the caterpillars of the silk moth)   8. True   9. False (it was invented in Italy)
10. False (it's called a cockapoo)

## Quiz 2: Multiple Choice

1. A) Football   2. B) Big Foot   3. C) 149 million km
(92 million miles)   4. B) Arendelle   5. A) Peru   6. C) Donald Trump   7. B) Lava (while it's still underground, it's known as magma)
8. C) Greece   9. C) Australian dollar   10. B) Around 260

## Quiz 3: Odd One Out

1. Turtle   2. Waistcoat   3. Miami Black Sox   4. Spruce
5. Blubber   6. Trombone   7. Kenya   8. Wikipedia   9. *The Goat Prince* (although *The Frog Prince* is a fairytale)   10. Coyote

## Quiz 4: Spot the Mistake

1. C (although identical twins do have the same eye and hair colour, they have different fingerprints)   2. A (bacteria are actually one of Earth's oldest lifeforms, having been around about 3.5 billion years)
3. B (the first commercial light bulb was invented by Thomas Edison)
4. B (US presidential elections are held every 4 years)   5. B (Everest is a mountain in Asia)   6. A (Ra had the head of a falcon)   7. A (an area of land surrounded by sea on two sides is an isthmus; a seamount is an underwater mountain)   8. B (Brazil have never won the women's football World Cup)   9. A (humans and chimpanzees actually have roughly the same number of hairs on their bodies, but human hairs are much finer)   10. B (a mythical creature that is half human and half bull is a minotaur)

## Quiz 5: Fill in the Blanks

1. Tails   2. Kitchen sponge   3. Flint   4. 4.5 billion
5. Wolves   6. Baikal   7. *Pokémon*   8. Salt (it's where we get the word 'salary' from)   9. Seven (North America, South America, Europe, Africa, Asia, Oceania, Antarctica)   10. Boomerang

## Quiz 6: Fruity Confusion

1. Apple   2. Kiwi fruit   3. Coconut   4. Dragon fruit   5. Durian
6. Grapes   7. Mangosteen   8. Orange   9. Pear   10. Watermelon

## Quiz 7: Lucky Dip

1. B) Tennis   2. A) Black cats   3. B) 31   4. C) China
5. B) Seven (its name comes from *hepta*, the Greek for 'seven')
6. C) Shark   7. A) Dubai, UAE   8. C) Soles of the feet
9. A) November   10. A) Lodge

## Quiz 8: Random Reasoning

1. False (it's Madrid)   2. False (it's called a Joey)   3. True
4. True   5. False (it's based in Japan)   6. False (it's known as the Winter Solstice)   7. True   8. True   9. False (some comets come close enough to Earth that they – and their long tails – can be seen in the night sky without a telescope)   10. False (although they look similar, there are several differences between crocs and gators)

## Quiz 9: What Vehicle Am I?

1. Helicopter   2. Hot-air balloon   3. Skateboard   4. Fire engine
5. Fork-lift truck   6. Rowing boat   7. Bicycle   8. Train
9. Tractor   10. Racing car

## Quiz 10: Adults vs Kids

**Adults**: 1. B) Eleven (the record is shared by *Ben Hur* in 1960, *Titanic* in 1968 and *Lord of the Rings: The Return of the King* in 2004)
2. C) Holocene (it's the period we're living in now)
3. B) 305 cm (10 ft)   4. True (the female calls 'twit' and the male answers 'twoo')   5. A) Mount St. Helens

**Kids**: 1. B) Los Angeles   2. C) Dodo   3. A) Badminton   4. True (it reflects the light which makes it look white)   5. A) Krakatoa

# CHAPTER 10: WEIRD BUT TRUE

## Quiz 1: True or False

1. False (it actually has around 40,000 muscles in its trunk; in contrast, there are only around 600 muscles in the whole of you)    2. True    3. True (some species can wriggle their bodies through the air to glide between trees)    4. False (the wingspan of the largest moth in the world, the Atlas moth, can reach 30 cm)    5. True (scientists think the pink colour of the water is caused by a type of algae)    6. True (reindeer can reach 80 kph while even an Olympic sprint champion can only reach 45 kph)    7. False (male proboscis monkeys have extremely long noses)    8. True (the plants form spongy masses on hillsides which from afar look like sheep)    9. False (they can spin their heads most of the way round, 270°)    10. True (it may sound unbelievable, but the jellyfish is able to regenerate itself at the end of its life and start its lifecycle all over again)

## Quiz 2: Multiple Choice

1. B) Cat    2. B) Tug of War    3. C) Agatha Christie    4. A) Coffee
5. C) Mali (his fortune was based on gold mining)    6. C) Five (English, German, French, Italian and Latin)    7. C) Flamingos    8. C) 217 years
9. B) Fork    10. B) Burns

## Quiz 3: Odd One Out

1. Snake beetle    2. Smelly sock plant    3. Unicorn racing
4. Frying pan    5. Giraffe shark    6. Floating sofa    7. Wind-powered skateboard    8. Poached slugs    9. Albatross    10. Candyfloss Festival

## Quiz 4: Spot the Mistake

1. B (pineapples don't grow on trees; they grow on short plants)
2. C (cheese has been around since ancient times)    3. B ('biscuit' comes from a French word meaning 'twice-baked' because biscuits were originally cooked two times before being eaten)    4. A (pasta is made from a mix of flour, water and eggs – it doesn't grow on trees)
5. B (the first McDonald's restaurant opened in 1948)    6. C    7. B
8. B    9. A (the scientific name for chocolate, *theobroma cacao*, actually translates as 'food of the gods')    10. C (cranberries are fruits)

## Quiz 5: Fill in the Blanks
1. The Eiffel Tower  2. Pebbles  3. Single-decker bus  4. One week (over a week, in fact)  5. Tree (a 150-year-old oak tree)  6. Head  7. Australia  8. 1971  9. Microwave  10. Yodels

## Quiz 6: Curious Creatures
1. Anglerfish  2. Blobfish  3. Dumbo octopus  4. Goblin shark  5. Handfish  6. Leafy Sea Dragon  7. Manta ray  8. Pufferfish  9. Sea cucumber  10. Sea pen

## Quiz 7: Culture Vultures
1. C) Sydney  2. B) 2012  3. C) £4 million (it was made of solid gold)  4. A) *Hamilton*  5. B) Denmark  6. A) Sea snails  7. B) Jessie  8. C) Horses  9. A) Asteroid  10. A) 3.8 km (2.4 miles)

## Quiz 8: Out of this World
1. True (its south pole has been measured at −240°C, colder than Pluto)
2. False (there are countless billions of stars)  3. False (it's located on Venus and is nine times longer than Earth's Grand Canyon)
4. False (it takes Neptune a whopping 165 years to orbit the Sun)
5. True (by 11-year-old Venetia Burney)  6. True (Venus spins so slowly, it completes an orbit of the Sun before it completes a rotation on its axis)  7. True  8. False (although they have left lots of other things, including golf balls)  9. True (Scientists think that pressure in Jupiter's atmosphere hardens carbon into diamonds which then falls like rain)  10. True (there's no wind or water to wash them away)

## Quiz 9: Who or What Am I?
1. Wombat  2. White House  3. Tutankhamun  4. Okapi  5. Elizabeth I  6. International Space Station  7. 'Happy Birthday'  8. *Mona Lisa*  9. Canada  10. Pigeon

## Quiz 10: Adults vs Kids
**Adults:** 1. A) Shrew  2. C) Pineal gland  3. B) Pye Corner  4. True  5. A) Duck (because it was originally played with a live duck)

**Kids:** 1. B) Moths  2. C) Nerve cells  3. B) 1616  4. True  5. A) Silver (coated with a thin layer of gold)

# NOTES
# AND
# SCRIBBLES

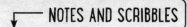

# ALSO AVAILABLE:

ISBN 9781780558882

ISBN 9781780559155

ISBN 9781780558738

ISBN 9781780558264

ISBN 9781780558721

ISBN 9781780557403

ISBN 9781780556642

ISBN 9781780556635

ISBN 9781780556628

ISBN 9781780556543

ISBN 9781780556659

ISBN 9781780556192

ISBN 9781780556208

ISBN 9781780556185

ISBN 9781780555935

ISBN 9781780555638

ISBN 9781780554730

ISBN 9781780555621

ISBN 9781780554723

ISBN 9781780555409

ISBN 9781780553146

ISBN 9781780553085

ISBN 9781780553078

ISBN 9781780552491